Julia Fox

Biography

Beneath the Glitz

Table of Contents

Chapter 1: The American Dream

Chapter 2: Big Girl

Chapter 3: Motherland

Chapter 4: Homecoming Fiend

Chapter 5: Aftershock

Chapter 6: Mastermind

Chapter 7: Billion-Dollar Baby

Chapter 8: PTSD

Chapter 9: Starstruck

Chapter 10: A Parting Gift

Chapter 11: Sudden Starfall

Chapter 1:
THE AMERICAN DREAM

It's 1996, and I've just arrived in the magnificent city of New York City. I drop my suitcase and cross myself the instant we walk off the plane and my small feet strike the ground. "Grazie a Dio," I say quietly to myself. During the plane flight, I asked my father, "Will we all die if the plane crashes?" He casually said, "Duh." The rest of the journey was spent in solitary prayer, my gaze riveted on the foreboding, limitless ocean beneath us. Despite my basic command of the English language, I prefer to communicate in my home tongue. I was born in Italy and have spent the last few years in Saronno, a little town in the province of Varese, where the city resembles the ruins of a once-charming little town. But I look beyond the shabby graffiti that covers the pastel pink walls. It's home to me.

I'm not new to this big metropolis. I've been here more times than I can remember. I was two months old the first time we traveled across the Atlantic to see my father's family. I even lived here for a bit before the disaster. However, today feels like the first time. It's as if I'm seeing this place for the first time. And, given the debacle of the previous attempt, this is a new beginning, a chance to start over.

It's early September, and the air is thick with humidity, clinging to my skin like a lovely sticky veil. As soon as I step outdoors, a flood of activity hits me, overwhelming all of my senses. Everyone is quite loud, and they are not at all courteous. Whether they're welcoming each other or urging each other to "Get the fuck out of the way," they make a point of causing a commotion. I wave to the weird individuals passing by, and they look at me, perplexed and alarmed. "Do I know you?!" exclaims one woman. My father yanks me away and urges me to stop. This will be a difficult habit to break. I can't imagine walking past someone without acknowledging them; it's impolite. But I don't say anything out loud; I keep my thoughts to myself. I just nod, trying to take in as much information as possible to ease this adjustment. He deserves it.

My father, like a magician, summons a yellow taxi cab with a sweep of his palm. He throws my little red suitcase, which was filled with my most valuable items, into the trunk, and I get onto the cracked and cigarette-smoked brown leather seats. My father gives him the location, and the driver, who is wearing a turban and aviator sunglasses, blows a heavy cloud of smoke. "Fifty bucks."

As we drive through the boroughs in silence on our approach to Manhattan, I note how all of the signs advertising movies include guns and violence. And, oddly, there are no naked ladies. It's completely normal in Italy to look up at a billboard and have a large pair of bronzed oily tits offer you sunscreen at eight a.m. on a January morning.

Everything is massive here. The tall structures cast shadows as far as my big eyes can see, while the people, who don't appear alike, scurry around as if in some grand dance. I'm a country girl from a little town where everything appears to be miniature in comparison. I, too, feel small, but not in an insignificant sense. I feel small in an exhilarating sense, as if I have yet to be discovered.

As the automobile crawls through the gridlocked rush-hour streets, the journey seems interminable. I squirm in the backseat, fidgeting with my bracelet, a gold nameplate that reads "Giulia," which was placed on my wrist at birth. The numerous lanes and big sea of automobiles overwhelm me. I believe there are too many options. I feel shivers just thinking about becoming lost in this concrete maze. I swallow the thought and ignore the reality that I'm beginning to feel insignificant and unimportant. Perhaps even a bother.

We finally arrive at a huge structure, its rusty gray brickwork ornamented with scaffolding and an emerald-green awning with large tarnished bronze letters. The glass doors slide open, revealing a cheerful man with a mustache anxious to assist my father with the suitcases. "Javier, this is Julia, my daughter." She's going to be here for a while!" Javier extends his hand and says, "Hola, Hoolia." I laugh. I'd never heard my name uttered like that before.

"Before I forget, this is your address now, if you ever get lost." My father indicates the green street signs on the corner. He's already gone inside the building before I can read them. Because I'm continuously jogging behind my dad to keep up, I can tell he's not used to having kids around.

He calls the elevator once inside, and after a few seconds of waiting, he becomes impatient and leads me up the service stairs. I follow him down the long, winding corridor all the way to Apartment 2F. He swings open the door without first unlocking it and exclaims, "We're home!", "You don't lock the door?" I ask, surprised. He shrugs and says, "We've got nothing of value here." How about me? I'm thinking to myself. I don't really trust him, but I don't have any other choice. I accept his response and instantly turn my attention to my new home.

The room is covered in plastic sheets to protect the furniture from paint splatter, and the paint smell is strong, but the sunlight coming in through the windows fills the space with warmth.

My father, beaming with delight, gives me a great tour of the place. It's not particularly large, yet it feels enormous to me. I've never lived in a house with a hallway. "I saved the best for last... your very own bedroom!" he says as we reach the end of the corridor. He pushes the door open to reveal a man in a beret casually painting clouds on the ceiling from atop a ladder!

My pupils dilate as a flush sweeps across my cheeks. I've never seen anything that beautiful in my life! But basically, I'm happy to have my own room like the kids on TV.

I never had the luxury of privacy at my grandfather's house. Actually, I was never alone. We were literally on top of each other, crowded into the same cramped one-bedroom apartment where my mother had grown up. My brother and I shared the living room with Grandpa, and when our mother was home, he slept on the pullout couch in her room with her. But she was rarely home before nightfall. She worked as a nurse and was studying to be a psychologist, and she had little money, two small children, and a certifiably mad baby daddy a thousand miles away, so I couldn't blame her for staying up late.

We were homeless the last time I was in New York. That's unclear how that happened, but I recall bouncing around between the homes of various family members and friends. The fighting, confusion, and tears are indelible in my mind. The worst location we stayed was in Chinatown, in a dark squat house with around twenty people sleeping on mats all over the floor. While I was sleeping, a battle broke out, and when I awoke in the morning, there was a thick puddle of what appeared to be blood on the floor near the entrance. My father quickly grabbed me up and we went away on his bicycle, never to return. We never talked about it again.

Following that, we began sleeping on my father's job sites. One of them was a lovely Upper West Side townhouse with arched entrances and a fireplace. It was Christmastime, and the owners asked my father to complete a partial restoration while they were away on vacation. They had no idea my father had moved us all in on the first day of work. At first, everything went swimmingly, and my parents even cuddled on the couch by the fire in the evenings as the snow piled up outside. It didn't matter to me that it wasn't technically our home. It was great fun pretending, and I was simply glad we were all finally together.

I'm happy to be in New York with my father, yet a part of me misses my grandfather. He hardly left the house after my grandmother died, and we were his entire world. Instead of spending his golden years in peace, he was left to raise two wild children on his own. He'd make us dinner and pick us up from school. We'd get on the back of his motorcycle and go to the garden, where we'd grab grapes from the vines and stuff them into our mouths. We even planted a pine tree one summer and saw it blossom and get taller year after year. He'd proudly frame and place my sketches on the wall, making care to point them out to the few people we had over. "Hai visto l'artista?" he'd ask, a bright smile on his face. We'd sit in a circle and say our prayers aloud before he sang us the same stanza of the only lullaby he knew until we fell asleep.

"When is Mamma and Christopher coming?" In shaky English, I ask my father. Without looking up from his beeper, he says, "Soon, sweetie." I'm not convinced by this response, but before I can enquire further, he grabs my hand and walks me next door. "I'd like you to meet someone." They've also recently relocated."

My father comes to the door and knocks. The TV is spewing loud sounds, but there is no response. When he tries again, a woman's piercing wail echoes through the walls. It's not your average scream; it's something out of a horror movie. I looked up at my father, questioning if we should leave, but he seemed entirely unconcerned.

We heart beating and pumping until the door cracks open, and a tiny guy with shaggy dirty-blonde hair, baggy UFO pants, and a bizarre blue growth on his nose steps into the doorway. I make an effort not to stare at it. A massive, gigantic golden retriever approaches from behind him, pushing his way through. He struggles to keep the dog inside until a woman with long bleached blonde hair appears and wrestles the dog inside.

"Oh, hellooo!" Julia, you must be! Your father was telling us all about you! My name is Sharon. It's a pleasure to meet you! Say hello to Julia, Josh!"

Her voice is loud and noisy, and she speaks with a heavy New York drawl, but she's warm and odd, and I'm immediately drawn to her. "Hey," Josh says, his face impish and his smirk far beyond his years. He's only four years old, and ordinarily I wouldn't associate with someone younger than me, but as I scan the room, taking in all the black leather and marble accents, I see he owns every video game console on the market.

Sharon spends the majority of her time in her room, either on the phone or in bed, watching her favorite shows. I overheard my father refer to her as a "JAP"-a Jewish American princess. Whatever that entails. She does not practice law despite having a law degree. Instead, she floats in and out of the building, stopping at drugstores and having brief walks with the dog. She always brings something to eat back, generally pizza or McDonald's Happy Meals. The only time she doesn't go out is when she gets a chemical peel, which turns her into a monster for a week.

Sharon and Josh live on Long Island and in Manhattan. When they come to town, I normally stay at their house. And when they come to Long Island, I normally stay at their house. I sneak out of my bedroom window and scale the scaffolding that encircles the structure. I jump onto their balcony and press my sweating palms against the glass until the window opens. I play video games, watch MTV, and eat the delectable cans of Chef Boyardee that they leave behind. It's far superior to the Hamburger Helper my father serves at our flat.

Sneaking into Sharon's wardrobe and modeling all of her outfits in the mirror is my favorite part. She owns a plethora of stunning fur coats, miniskirts, tube tops, and sensual leather jackets. I put them on and chat to myself in the mirror, pretending to be her.

While going through her drawers, I come across two ID cards with quite different birthdays, neither of which corresponds to the age she claimed I was, twenty-five. When I discover a slew of Polaroids of her when she was younger, backstage at various rock gigs dressed like a groupie, my mind is blown. When Josh and I aren't playing video games, we're usually getting into mischief. Sometimes it's harmless, like releasing our neighbors' cats by slashing their window screen apart, or throwing pennies down the rooftop until someone phones the cops. At times, we act like juvenile delinquents. As the complaints from the neighbors began to pour in, one lady in particular seemed to be offended by our antics.

Josh is the ideal substitute little brother for me, filling the emptiness left by the loss of my biological brother, Chris. I couldn't have asked for a finer interim replacement. We spend so much time together that we start fighting like brothers and sisters. He smacks me across the face with a baseball bat for no apparent reason, exactly like a real brother.

We only have one TV in the house, which my father uses to watch movies, but I worked out how to get basic cable by connecting some cables I found in the hallway. When I'm home alone, I spend hours watching Jerry Springer and Maury. All of the sleazy characters on the shows fascinate me. They have an irresistible mind-numbing element. As I zone out to the cacophony, I get a sense of tranquility. My father never allowed me to watch "daytime television." He claims that "it rots your brain." He'd be furious if he knew that all I did in Italy was sit in front of my grandfather's ancient television set with headphones on and a bowl of sugar, using a lighter to produce caramel clusters to suck on.

I've been snatching anything I can get my hands on lately. I go to the local stores and no one ever suspects me. I'm slick. I'm never caught. I steal chocolates from the dollar store, makeup from the drugstore, and clothes from my building's laundry room. When my father's wallet is out, I grab a tiny quantity of money and hide it in the secret compartment of my music box. It's not much, maybe a few hundred dollars here and there. Occasionally, fifty. Occasionally, five. But it rapidly adds up. However, I can only count to ninety-nine. So I create mounds of $99 until there are so many that I need to find a new spot to hide them.

I understand that stealing is unethical, but the security it provides me is priceless. My parents' incessant squabbles over money have left an unforgettable imprint on my mind. I swear I'll never be like them. I'm going to be wealthy when I grow up.

My father works a lot and is often weary and in a terrible attitude when he gets home. The silver lining is that, for the first time in my life, I have some independence and am beginning to shape a new identity. I feel like a small lady, the housewife. When we run out of toilet paper, I go to the dollar store and buy a roll. Because my father rarely goes grocery shopping, I fetch us some cereal and milk. I'm quickly figuring out how to take care of myself. My father walks in to get me dressed for school one morning, only to discover that I've already done so. I take my foot away from him as he bends over to knot my shoelace. "I do it myself."

If he's not too weary when he gets home from work, I'll hop on his handlebars and ride to Central Park, where we gather fireflies in mason jars and make wishes as we release them back into the night. In those moments, I believe I have the best father on the planet. On other nights, we head downstairs to the video store and rent a VHS movie. He occasionally lets me watch a movie with him, but if it's for adults, he orders me to go to bed. Despite the fact that I should be sleeping, I slip out of bed and watch the movie from the corner of the hallway.

When my father is not working, we go to the diner and order our favorite meal: a cream cheese omelet with home fries and buttered toast with strawberry jam. Later, he seats me at the dining room table and begins teaching me how to read and write in English. Despite my efforts to squeeze my tongue between my teeth and blow, I have difficulty pronouncing "th," which sounds like "d" to him. He loses his patience so quickly, and I'm getting itchy and bored. I wish I had the ability to watch Jerry Springer.

I weep myself to sleep at night. I use my plush animals to block the sounds since I don't want him to wake up. He's particularly grumpy. I'm doing my best to be a big girl, but I miss my mom and brother terribly. And I greatly miss my grandfather's comfort.

My father frequently drops me off at my grandmother Margaret's apartment. He describes her as a "wannabe WASP," whatever that implies. She lives in a studio apartment ten streets away at an old home. She has the softest pearly white hair and the same huge blue eyes that I inherited. She lets me apply her makeup and give her facials despite the fact that I have no idea what I'm doing. She enjoys classical music, costume jewelry, her numerous plants, her elderly pets, and the arts. She makes certain that I learn the proper way to speak and that I always use proper etiquette. "May I" rather than "Can I," and "yes" rather than "yeah."

She has a large collection of art supplies and encourages me to be creative. We spend hours watercoloring in Central Park, and when we return home, she hangs my painting on the wall, just like

Grandpa. She brings me to the Met, the Natural History Museum, the Whitney, and the MoMA. She points out the beauty all around us as we walk. She takes me to the opera, theater, and ballet. And, despite the fact that we never have decent seats, she always remembers to bring two pairs of binoculars for us. I never look at the stage because I'm too busy spying on the audience members. I enjoy people-watching. I'm curious about who these folks are, what their lives are like, and whether or not they're having fun. Many of them appear to be sleeping. Grandma doesn't mind if I'm distracted. She wears a perpetual smile on her face at all times.

My aunt Beth is always close by, trailing behind us with many tote bags. They make fun of her for being Grandma's shadow. "We're attached at the hip," Beth chuckles. And, because my grandmother is in a wheelchair due to having polio as a child, this setup is ideal for her. What about Beth? I'm not convinced, but she doesn't seem to mind.

During disagreements with my father, I overhear my mother making disparaging remarks about my grandmother and Beth, claiming that they are mentally sick and so he is as well. I'm wondering if that implies I'll get sick as well. Beth casually tells Grandma a story her therapist told her one day. Grandma raises her head from her paper, her mood swings abruptly, and her gaze narrows toward Beth. "Call her up and fire her." I put down my work and focus on the issue, which is becoming increasingly unpleasant. "Oh, Mom, I don't want to fire her. She's been a huge assistance to me. "I was able to connect with her."

Beth's pleadings are ineffective, and my grandmother stiffens in her seat. "No. She should not be wasting your time by talking about herself. "Call her right now and fire her."

My aunt Beth, defeated, sighs and asks, "Well, what do you want me to say?"

"Tell her that she's not the right fit for your particular needs," my grandmother responds, irritated. My aunt gives me a nod. As she reaches for the receiver, her hand trembles. She reluctantly enters her therapist's phone number. Beth is the center of attention. This interaction had even the cat's ears perked up. Before she gets the answering machine, the phone rings a few times. I breathed a sigh of relief. She struggles to get the words out of her mouth.

"It... it was wonderful meeting you, but my mother and I just don't think you're the right fit for me." It's not a personal attack. You were fantastic. Thank you very much for your time."

She hangs up the phone, looking as if she's ready to cry.

"Don't worry, sweetheart," Grandma adds, her tone softening and softening, "we are going to find you someone much better."
I'm too young to really appreciate what I just watched, but it has irrevocably altered my perception of their relationship.

My father tells me to get ready because I'll be starting school soon. As I dread the concept, my palms begin to sweat heavily. My hands are usually clammy because I suffer from hyperhidrosis. He drags me to Modell's and insists on buying me the most hideous pair of brown Mary Janes. I stomp my foot and inform him that I want the gleaming blue ones. He claims they're too expensive, so I persuade him to get me a pair of red high-tops instead.

"Fine since they're only five bucks."

We're both pleased, and that night he brings me to see my first adult movie in a theater. I am completely blown away with The Fifth

Element. Milla Jovovich's hair and outfit leave an indelible imprint on my malleable small mind. She is quite attractive, and I aspire to be just like her when I grow up. On the ride home, I peppered my father with movie-related questions.

"Well, if you behave, maybe I'll put you in a movie!"

My mouth drops open. This man is truly my hero!

My father's good friend Nathan, it turns out, is developing a little independent film in Queens and has asked my father for a small investment. My father agreed to pay him the money if they found a role for me. That's show business, baby!

A few weeks later, I'm on the set of Fire Dancer, a film about a refugee who flees Afghanistan's turmoil only to commit suicide later. In one flashback, I am buried beneath the ruins of a war-torn village. It's hard work, and I don't even have any lines. It's all very monotonous and uninteresting. Not at all like the film The Fifth Element. This turns out to be one of my father's many terrible investments since, after the film was completed, I believe there was some sort of financial disagreement that resulted in Nathan being found guilty of murdering the director of Fire Dancer. His severed body parts were found in a suitcase on a random Queens street. As you can expect, this caused a significant delay in the finishing of the film because both the producer and the director were permanently out of commission. A few years later, we received an invitation in the mail to the Tribeca Film Festival premiere of Fire Dancer. We decided to go see it anyway. They omitted my section.

I painstakingly packed my backpack the night before my first day of school. I consider everything: a sharpener, an eraser, a jar of colored pencils so large that it won't fit in my rucksack. I go down on my knees right before bed and beg God to kindly keep an eye on me, as I often do when I'm worried. I miss my mother and grandfather more than ever.

I get ready in the morning before my father gets up. I find the lone matching pair of socks and tuck my shirt in like all the kids in Italy. I brush my hair and tuck it nicely behind my ears. He walks in, clearly impressed and relieved to find me prepared. All I want is for today to be great. There were no hiccups. My sweating hands hold the large jar of colored pencils on my lap as my father cycles me to school. I take in every second before we get at the massive black doors. I hop off his handlebars and feel tears well up in my eyes as I urge him not to leave yet, imploring him to come inside with me.

He fixes his gaze on me. "Enjoy it now, 'cause it's all downhill from here, kid." He's already biked away before I can respond. I drag my feet inside the building, defeated and perplexed, and eventually find my classroom. But not before tripping and spilling the full jar of colored pencils on the floor as soon as I enter through the doorway. One specific girl laughs a little too loudly at my accident, and I immediately want to punish her. I grab my pencils as quickly as I can and race to a seat in the back, where I'm instructed that we're only allowed to use pens in this session because the teacher wants to "see our mistakes." I can feel the tears welling up once more. I withdraw to my corner and check out. I start scribbling when the same girl who laughed at me comes around and says, "My name is Mia." "Can you tell me your name?" I reply, "Julia," and return to my doodling. I still don't have faith in her.

Later, around lunchtime, I noticed her staring at me. She seems to want to befriend me the more I push her away. I'm hungry, but when I unzip my lunch box, it stinks. "Ew, what's that smell?!" someone exclaims, and I hastily close the door. My father must have created his own tuna fish sandwich. This is the same man who scrapes mold from old food and then consumes it. This is the same man that dumpster dives and eats from garbage cans. I'm fighting back tears, so embarrassed, when Mia, who I've decided cannot read social cues, eventually stops buzzing around and says, "Wanna see something cool?"

I trail her out of the cafeteria and down an empty corridor. She comes to a halt in front of a vending machine and says, "Okay, be on the lookout." She inserts her long, lanky arm inside and up the spout, effectively knocking down a Twix bar. She uses her teeth to rip it open and hands me one. "Now it's your turn!" I accept the challenge and grab a pack of Skittles in one fast motion.

When my father gets me up from after-school, we head to a nearby diner for hot chocolate with extra whipped cream. Myself, Mia, my father, and Marissa. We go so frequently that it has become a ritual. It also becomes the most anticipated aspect of my day. Mia suggests that I purchase a computer so that we can communicate via AOL. When my father gets home from work, I urge him to get one for me. He informs me, as expected, "I don't have the money for it." I've decided to part ways with my stolen security fund. I dash to fetch my music box from under my mattress and proudly present him with the hundreds of piles of $99 I've amassed. He counts it and is astounded to see that it is sufficient for TWO computers.

I hug my father and phone Mia to inform her of the news. Marissa answers the phone and requests to talk with my father. He snatches the phone and pushes me away. I stand at the entrance, intrigued as to what they may possibly be discussing. I overheard him say, "I love you, too." I'm perplexed, but I don't think much of it when he returns an hour later with a brand-new computer from P. C. Richard & Son. Later that night, after we figured out how to connect to AOL, we set up my first email address. Because "Poshspice" is already used, I settle with "gingerkitty123."

Mia and I will exist as sisters for the next two years. We take my father's boat out on the Hudson River and fearlessly dive into the murky water. Marissa exclaims, but my father assures her that it is beneficial to my immune system. In the winter, we go ice skating at Chelsea Piers, and in the summer, we go to Coney Island's beach, where we stand on our parents' toes to meet the height limit for the rides. We're known at school as "The Sleepover Sisters," because we all go home together every night. The Parent Trap is one of our favorite movies because we identify so strongly with Lindsay Lohan's characters.

My father frequently pays a visit to Marissa's. He also spends the night on occasion. And some nights, they go out together alone, leaving us at home with the babysitter. Our squabbling becomes so terrible that one of the babysitters quits mid shift, leaving us alone for the rest of the night. Another tells our parents that our poor behavior has traumatized her. The truth is that we spend far too much time together and could benefit from a break. We never get a night off now that our parents are pals.

While our parents are away, we watch Romy and Michele's High School Reunion three times in a row and decide we want to be just like them when we grow up. "My name is Mary!" "You're Rhoda!" I exclaim. "No. "I'm Mary!" she responds.

Marissa arrives home alone, without my father. She sits beside us on the pullout couch and begins braiding our hair. She appears pensive until she asks me, "How would you feel if you had a little brother?" I pause for a second and tell her I already have a younger brother and don't want another. She gives a nod. I realize this is an odd question, but I dismiss it. I frequently assume Marissa to be my mother. She's nurturing and warm, yet she also has a fiery wild side. She likes to go out at night, wears red lipstick, and dances naked in the mirror. I'm not surprised when I discover her naked Polaroids while searching through some old boxes in her loft.

She buys us outfits and has us play dress-up. She shows me how to apply nail paint and lipstick and even watches me shave my legs, prepared with a Band-Aid in case I hurt myself. She teaches me appropriate hygiene and how to brush and part my hair perfectly with the tip of a comb. She allows us to watch TV and does not scold us when we eat cookies after brushing our teeth. She kisses us each on the forehead before bed and tells us how much she loves us. She does everything my mother would never do, but she isn't my mother. That area has been claimed, for better or worse.

I came in one evening to find my father sitting on the edge of his bed, with Marissa standing beside him. I stand still in the doorway, watching him pull her close to him by the waist. She leans in and whispers something into his ear before kissing him on the lips.

I exhale and flee the room. It's not right, I know. I'm not sure what I'm feeling; it's a new experience for me: the biting sting of betrayal. I lock myself in the bathroom and contemplate how I'm going to deal with this. Everything is clear now. Marissa would wait until we were sound asleep before slithering out of bed and slipping into the darkness during our regular sleepovers. I was curious about where she was heading but never thought to inquire. I'm pretty sure she was going to sleep in my father's room. How could I have been so naive as to believe it was harmless?! I'm embarrassed.

I force the unpleasant feelings away, but the image of them kissing is burnt in my mind, and I wish I hadn't seen it. I wish I could go back in time and erase that chapter of my life, but I can't. The next day, I finally snap and resolve to face him. "I saw you kiss Marissa!" I yell, standing in the corridor too outraged to approach him.

He begins to scramble for excuses. He stutters and cowers as he tries to fool me into thinking I didn't see what I know I did. He claims it was only a peck, a love tap, and nothing to be concerned about. "I love Mommy," he says, assuring me. I'm not convinced, but I made the intentional decision to accept his explanation because I don't have much of a choice. We continued to live this way until one of my mother's biannual trips to New York, when she discovered a pair of ripped pantyhose under my father's bed.

That particular morning, I chose to skip school and amazingly convinced my parents that I was too sick to go. That was a huge oversight. Armed with the evidence, my mother faced my father, who attempted to persuade her that the pantyhose belonged to her. "I would never wear this cheap brand with all these holes in it!" said my mother without hesitation. She was enraged. Her face was bright red, and her jaw twitched like it did when she was about to strike.

She backed my father into a corner by yanking every glass picture frame off the wall, one by one, and slamming it over his head. Then she went to the kitchen cupboards and started pulling out wine glasses and glass dishes, tossing them at him. We were swimming in a sea of glass, and I began to worry about my father. I dashed across the shards, standing between them, pleading with her to stop. He took advantage of the situation to depart the apartment, most likely to Marissa's place. My mother went back into her room and began sobbing.

I trailed behind her, attempting to console her, but she was distraught. She asked me if I knew through the flood of tears. I was very embarrassed. I nodded and kept my look low. When I told her what I witnessed, she assured me that everything was fine and that it wasn't my fault, but I know a small part of her despised me for it. I'd deceived her in the worst possible way.

I pick bits of glass out of my feet over the next two days as she silently dumps every picture of Mia and me in the trash. She also gets rid of any toys, books, stuffed animals, or anything that reminds her of Mia and Marissa. She withdraws me from school and enrolls me in another local school before returning to Italy. I made one more phone call to Mia.

"My mom says I'm not allowed to see you anymore," I mutter quietly into the receiver, hoping no one hears me. Mia is mostly silent, as if someone is listening in on her conversation. I'm hoping she'll say anything, anything, but she doesn't. I'm frustrated that she doesn't make an effort to help me feel better. Before I hang up, I tell her that when we're older, we'll find each other and live in our own apartment, just like Romy and Michele. She laughs. I'm optimistic. She then hangs up the phone. I get off the phone.

My brother moves to America to live with us a few months later, and I'm not as thrilled as I expected to be. I don't want to downgrade after two years of having my own room, decorating it, and making it personal. I just want to return to my fantasy life. My brother and the neighbor, Josh, become best friends. They're now playing together without me, and I'm irritated. My retaliation is to dress them up like girls and use them as support dancers when I put on shows in the living room.

Even though I pick on my brother, I enjoy having him around. At the very least, I'm no longer alone at home, and Chris is a great listener. He's bright and inquisitive, and he actually enjoys hearing the stories I spend all night crafting. I can see he loves hearing my words come to life. He asks meaningful questions and gives insightful remarks as I read. When he's upset, I can hear him softly concealing his tears. He believes I have what it takes to become a true writer eventually.

My father has me compose poems in return for anything I want. Is that a new stuffed animal? "That will cost you fifty poems," he explains. "And they better be good, no haikus!" I recite my work to my brother to ensure that it satisfies our father's expectations. My father submits his favorite poems to poetry journals, and when they are published, he proudly bursts into our room, waving the book in my face. "See how talented you are?" he wonders. He never does this to my brother.

My new school is substantially larger than my old one. My previous school had an average of ten students per class, but this one has nearly thirty. I appreciate how I can just blend in with the crowd and daydream. I spend the majority of my time alone, sucking my thumb, biting my nails, humming made-up tunes, and twirling my hair, tucked away in a remote corner painting pictures of Mia and happier times. I obsessively scribble her birthday and zodiac sign ("Leo") all over my books so I don't forget. "Julia + Mia 4ever"

I write her long, detailed letters about my days and how lost I am without her, knowing I would never be able to send them. I'm not paying attention in class. I don't question the teachers or interact with the other pupils. They refer to me as "weirdo" and "freakazoid." They mock my accent and the way I speak. I don't have much clothing because my father never takes me shopping, and they tease me for wearing the same outfit every day. One of the girls gestures to my shoes and exclaims, "Ha ha! She's wearing fake Payless sneakers!" I begin to wonder if they are correct. Perhaps I am a freak. But I don't really care. I prefer to live in my fantasy world, away from reality. After what occurred to me the last time, I have no desire to make new acquaintances. I'm too enraged.

My unusual behavior catches the notice of my instructors, who notify the school therapist, who then notifies a social worker that I'm exhibiting worrying signals. At first, I'm ecstatic about being pulled out of class for an hour or two every day. The lady with the wild white curling hair inquires about my background. I tell her about Italy and my grandfather, and how much I wish I could return home. While she takes notes on a yellow pad, I sip on cherry cough drops. "Do your parents get angry at each other?" I twitch in my seat. "My dad says my mom has mad cow disease." After a few encounters with the social workers, I understand these aren't typical meetings. They appear to be asking me increasingly complicated questions that I don't want to answer, so I should get my act together and start acting regularly.

My father becomes aware of my actions and enrolls me in Transcendental Meditation lessons. I'm not sure what this implies, but I overheard him saying to the instructor, "Her teachers said she needed ADHD medication!" 'Fuck that, I'm not providing narcotics to a nine-year-old!' I exclaimed. "Her brain isn't even finished developing!"

I'm not sure why I require drugs. Perhaps I'm sick. I can't even remember the last time my father took me to the doctor.
In the Transcendental Meditation classes, I am the youngest participant. We discuss and meditate once a week in the evenings. My favorite part is listening to these unusual folks chat about grown-up topics. Their desires and anxieties, their vulnerabilities and flaws. This is even better than observing people at the opera with Grandma. We all have one thing in common, no matter how diverse we are: we just want to feel better.

My scribbles begin to fade in school, and I gradually shift my seat to the front of the class, raising my hand and asking questions. For the first time, I'm actually eager to study. I interact with the environment around me. I also get picked on less. My classmates begin to warm up to me, and I finally forget Mia's birthday and zodiac sign. Even better, I made a new best buddy. Danielle is her name. Danny is her given name.

Danny's parents are divorced, and her mother, Tanya, attends Alcoholics Anonymous, which sounds similar to my meditation classes-people simply sitting about and talking-but it doesn't appear to be working as well for her. Tanya is stunning, but she is severely damaged. She smells strongly like cloves and Chanel No. 5. Her paranoia and anxiety rub off on everyone around her. She is originally from Texas and was raised in a Christian home. Her mother, she claims, was a terrible mean woman who struck her all the time for no reason. She escaped as a teenager, severed all connections with her family, boarded a bus to New York City, and has been living on her own ever since. When Danny and I moan about school, mother tells us how fortunate we are since she did not have the same possibilities.

My mother despises anyone I bring around her, so I'm always pleased when she returns to Italy. I finally feel like I can exhale and return to my role as the woman of the house. She acts as if she is in command of everything while she is here. She is unaware that she is no longer a part of our daily lives. My friends are also relieved when she departs because they like the lack of supervision that comes with sleepovers at my house. I don't enjoy having my friends over while my mom is in town because I never know what she'll do. She could start an argument with me out of nowhere and demand that my friends leave right once, or she may scream insults at my father loud enough for them to hear. Not to mention that my father treats me differently. He's chilly to me for no apparent reason. He is stricter, and the stress of her presence is transferred to me.

I do enjoy having my mother's friends over because I know she will be lovely and on her best behavior, and she will make all of my favorite things. However, as soon as they leave, the fighting begins. I miss her food when she's gone. When things were better, I would stay in the kitchen for hours, captivated by her cooking, instinctively memorizing every single recipe. I can't seem to get out of the house fast enough these days. She just doesn't seem to like me. And, to be honest, I'm not sure I like her very much either.

But if there's one thing I'm confident of, it's that she despises my father. She even despises his possessions. And he has a lot of stuff. He finds most of his belongings on the street or has them unloaded on him by inhabitants of the houses he renovates. The majority of it is garbage. Kitsch trinkets, empty photo albums, sour wine cartons, and old novels. He has mountains of things he doesn't use but keeps collecting. The objects are piled on top of one other, pouring out every crack and crevice in the flat. My mother goes through his stack of antiques and throws them out when he's gone. This devastates him and fuels his need to gather meaningless items that he somehow finds valuable. He alleges she destroyed the only copy of his father's book. He keeps bringing it up like a broken record. I am pleading with them to obtain a divorce.

I start hearing him on the phone at night as soon as she leaves. Our rooms are next to each other, and the walls are thin. I press my ear against the wall and hear him comfort Marissa and assure her that they will be together soon. When I approach him, he claims to be talking to my mother, but I'm aware of the time difference, and my mother would not be up at four a.m. talking to him. He simply cannot be truthful. My hero is revealing himself to be nothing more than another flawed human being. I think to myself how unfair it is that he still gets to see Marissa and Mia while I don't, despite the fact that I did nothing wrong. Why am I being penalized as a result of his actions? I am filled with fury at him for ruining my life. I've lost all regard for him. I'm nine years old and have emotionally and psychologically checked out of this household. When I get home, I lock myself in the bathroom with the hair dryer on to avoid hearing the horrible sounds. Unfortunately, I know I have a long way to go before I can physically check out, so I'll have to settle for survival mode for the next few years.

My father gradually unravels. He grows extremely agitated. I believe that parenting two children alone while maintaining an affair is too much for him, and I never know who I'll come home to. Sometimes he's amusing, compassionate, and easygoing, and other times he breaks a chair over my head for something as strange as refusing to read the Bible because he suddenly became religious. He has periods when he becomes obsessed with something specific. It may be a new song or a new business. He becomes hysterical, wide-eyed, and aggressive. He also insults my brother, who now addresses him by his first name. Belt beatings are commonplace.

I want to adore him, but I frequently wish he could simply be a jerk all the time. This way, I wouldn't have to fight with myself as much. By erecting an unbreakable barrier between us, I learn to navigate my way through shattered expectations and endless disappointments. Every time I let down my guard, I'm reminded of why I had my barriers up in the first place. It's practically hard for me to thrive in an unstable hostile atmosphere, especially because my own development is so entwined with his. I'm forced to confront the disturbing reality that the individuals we're expected to protect are sometimes the people we need to protect ourselves from.

Following the graduation ceremony, the boys form a line to arm-wrestle me, and I easily defeat them all while my father proudly records my victories on his camcorder. Danny doesn't have to wait long to find new buddies. And I do as well. We meet at our after-school dance class, where we try to avoid each other. We, too, believe we are witches, casting charms on each other from across the room.

My new pals and I hold séances in my bedroom, evoking the spirit of Nirvana's late frontman, Kurt Cobain. I have a picture of Kurt Cobain taped to my wall and fantasize about dying so that I might join him on the other side. "It's better to burn out than fade away," he said in his suicide note. I'm curious what he meant, not aware it was a lyric from a Neil Young song. I go over every word in his diaries and read all of his biographies. I listen to his music on LimeWire and discreetly weep at the pained lyrics, finally feeling seen.

We sneak a smoke here and there without actually inhaling it. As we become more self-aware, we begin to change our look in subtle ways. We trade in our Sketchers for worn-in Converse and begin wearing dark lipstick to class. During recess, we sit in a circle and paint each other's nails black while singing System of a Down.

On a sweltering September morning during my first week of sixth grade, I'm sitting in my humanities class when a jet slams into the World Trade Center, shattering the tranquil morning air. I discover when a student teacher enters our classroom on tiptoes and whispers something to my teacher. Instead of keeping this extremely sensitive information to himself, he immediately and without warning blurts it out to us, then continues writing on the board with no explanation. We puzzledly gaze around the room at each other. Maybe he was only kidding, I reason.

It's only when parents begin to rush into the building to take up their children that I realize something is seriously wrong. I'm wondering if my father will show up.

Eventually, the administrators summon us all to the auditorium, where we sit cross-legged and anxious for further information. I overheard a boy next to me say, "I heard there were two planes." What an odd coincidence that two planes would both crash on the same day, I suppose. The principle silences us with a solemn question: "Does anyone have a relative, parent, or family member who works at the World Trade Center?"

As a few small arms shoot up from the crowd, the room falls silent. "If you raise your hand, please come to the front of the room." A few tearful-eyed children stand up, their legs shaky as they weave through the mass of eyeballs. They make their way to the front and are led out of the auditorium, leaving a trail of weeping that can be heard for a long time.

The principal assures the remaining children that they should not be concerned and that our parents will pick us up soon. I attempt calling my father. There was no response. I begin to get concerned. My father does not work at the World Trade Center, but he is employed throughout the city. My thoughts begin to wander to a dark place, and I begin to wonder if he got a job downtown repairing an apartment, and if anything happened to him. I called him once again. There is no signal.

My friends are all picked up. It's now after three p.m., and I'm the final student standing. I'm sitting in the cafeteria, reading to take my mind off things. Finally, my father appears. I'm angry with him for causing me to be concerned. He tells me eagerly that as soon as the first plane struck, he grabbed his camera and took his boat out, going as close to the devastation as he could. I wish he had picked me up so I could have joined him.

On the way home, he says something about World War III, which I believe is exaggerated. There will be no school the next day. I go to Josh's, where every channel on TV repeats the same footage of buildings collapsing on themselves. I wish I could just ignore it, but I can't.

Sharon places a newspaper of the New York Post on the table, which features a photo of the attack and the words "ACT OF WAR" in bold black characters. I suppose my father wasn't exaggerating. This causes my palms to sweat. I wish we could go back in time.

9/11 throws me into maturity before the age of puberty and entirely dominates my life. The city is shrouded in a dense black cloud. The relics are strewn about: a burned book page, a woman's shoe, a snapshot, and a pair of broken sunglasses. The faces on the missing posters stare back at me blankly. There are so many of them, all piled on top of one another, each expressing a heartbreaking narrative. I lie in bed at night, wondering if every plane I hear flying overhead is a bomb. I clutch my pillow over my ears and brace myself for the blow.

Chapter 2:
BIG GIRL

I'm playing Pokémon cards next door with Chris and Josh when I feel an odd tingling in my pants. I'm sitting cross-legged on a folded newspaper when I notice small red droplets soaking through my jeans and onto the paper. Panic creeps in when I realize it's blood. I think about what to do next for a few moments. Part of me wants to say something, but the other part doesn't want them to know I'm not like them. I awkwardly rise up, clutching the newspaper to my buttocks, and sprint backwards home. Chris and Josh stare at me with bewildered expressions and continue playing unaffected.

I don't feel comfortable telling my father, so I call my mother. When I deliver her the news, her voice betrays her emotions. She assures me that she is not upset, yet her tone is sorrowful. "I just wasn't expecting this," she confesses. I can't get rid of the sensation that I did something wrong. My father locks her in the bathroom with me once my parents return home, forcing her to teach me how to correctly place a tampon in my vagina.

My father's words echo through the door as my mother desperately tries to open it. "Be a good mother!" he exhorts as I sweatily grasp the plastic applicator in my palms. She stops, attempting to conceal her obvious distress, then nonchalantly offers, "You should use pads."

I nod meekly, eager for this bizarre, forced meeting to be over. I appreciate my father's attempt to compel intimacy between us, but it's evident that she has no desire to conduct any mother activities. "Okay, she taught me how to do it!" I yell through the open door. My father lets go of the doorknob, and I hurry out of the restroom, my cheeks red with embarrassment.

Ella, my new friend, claims that her mother is her best friend. After school, I tell my mother that she is my best friend. She sighs and brushes me aside. "You sound so American." I realize this is meant to be an insult. "Mothers and daughters can't be 'friends.'" I can't help but think I'm missing out on something important in life.

Ella is the third and youngest of three sisters. Ella, Kat, and Kayla all live with Silvia, their mother, who divorced their father when he cheated on her. He ended up marrying his mistress, which is a really sensitive matter. On certain occasions, like their anniversary, she'll pull out images of his new bride, and we'll all have to tell Silvia in unison how ugly she is. The three sisters all have gorgeous thick auburn hair and huge green eyes. I have severe acne, but their skin is soft, smooth, and devoid of blemishes. They're tall, slim, and tanned. Everything I'm not, but for some reason they enjoy having me over.

Kayla, fortunately for me, has some behavioral issues and frequently gets into fights, so she spends a lot of time with wealthy family friends in New Jersey. This implies that there is generally a bed available for me. I start going to Ella's house every night, and before I know it, I'm almost the fourth sister.

Silvia is a heavy drinker. We even came home from school one day to discover her having sex with her drug dealer in the middle of the afternoon in the living room. We dash past them, covering our eyes, to Ella's chamber. Ella is unconcerned by the sight because she is accustomed to her mother's conduct. When they're finished, the dealer knocks on Ella's door and hands us a jar of nasty weed as compensation for our trouble. I've never smoked marijuana before, but Ella is an expert. She says she'll roll one up for us when she finishes her homework. Ella is quite concerned about school. She is seated near the front of the class. She extends her hand. She performs well on tests. She is everything I aspire to be. I stop coming home, which leads to me stopping meditating, and now I can't sit still. I lose concentration. I am chastised. I'm thrown out of class. I'm not sure why Ella is friends with me when she could be friends with the popular girls.

Ella downloads songs from LimeWire for us to listen to while Sublime plays on the computer. I'm mesmerized as I watch her roll a joint and light it up while delicately placing it to her finely puckered lips. She takes a few easy draws and hands it to me. My heartbeat is audible through my Playboy tank top. I'm doing my best to be calm.

I take a short breath and instantly expel the foul smoke. "You have to inhale or else you won't feel it," she says anxiously, her blue eyes turning bloodshot. I'm frightened of disappointing her, so I take a tiny inhale and instantly begin coughing excessively. Tears trickle down my cheeks till we both burst out laughing.

I enjoy being high. I'm feeling warm and fuzzy, and everything is hilarious. My ideas are becoming more organized, and I can now hear myself think. Ella demonstrates how to roll joints using a filter "like the French," as she puts it. We also kiss like the French on occasion. She swears it's only practice for the real thing, but I can tell she enjoys it. We play games like spin the bottle and seven minutes in heaven, then act as if nothing happened.

Her seventeen-year-old sister Kat has a live-in boyfriend named José. I constantly rummage through her things if I need to find a lighter in her room. I'm intrigued by this unusual, cool female. Her walls are appropriately black and filled with punk rock posters. Among the mayhem on the floor are penis-shaped straws, vibrating crotch toys, pink fuzzy handcuffs, plastic tiaras, and unknown substances coating every surface. Ella tells me she's a dominatrix and that she beats guys up for money, and I'm blown away by how much fun that sounds.

Kat always barges into Ella's room before work to check herself out in the full-length mirror. I sit by her feet, dressed in patent-leather platform Mary Janes, as she analyzes her reflection. Her lengthy legs seem to stretch for miles in her black fishnet stockings. She notices my ogling glance through the glass and says, slyly, "Do I look badass?" I shake my head wildly back and forth, shocked by her words, until Ella yells at her, "Can you get the fuck out of my room?"

Ella is incredibly interested in politics. Her enthusiasm is contagious as I learn more about the injustices perpetrated by our government. On a beautiful April morning, we skip school and board a bus bound for Washington, D.C., to take part in a sit-in against the Iraq war. We had spent the night before making cardboard signs to carry to the march. I swing my bedazzled "No Blood for Oil" banner around while Ella yells "Bring back our troops!" at the top of her lungs. The day is emotional, as we are almost arrested for lying down on the street, but the experience just pulls us closer together.

We decide to get our belly buttons pierced on Saint Mark's, taking turns on the phone outside pretending to be each other's mothers and duping the piercer. It becomes our little secret as we proudly show off our matching belly rings to our envious peers at school. I become addicted to the rush of the needle puncturing my flesh, and we quickly become regulars at the piercing station. I even get my tongue and lip pierced before the end of seventh grade, all while my father is completely unaware.

When Silvia is away, the apartment changes into a refuge for rainbow-haired freaks and leather-clad weirdos. Kat's buddies come over and blast Rage Against the Machine and break crap, but nobody cares except Ella, who does her best to keep it together. Skateboards are scattered across the floor, and the aroma of bong hits and cheap beer fills the air as I sit on the couch, viewing the mayhem.

Mikey, one of Kat's buddies, is a frequent visitor. He's covered in tattoos and has a scruffy boyish charm, despite his age. He buys us a large bottle of Jack Daniel's and advises us not to consume it too quickly. I'd never drank hard alcohol before, except for the rare sip of grappa my grandfather made me gargle whenever I had a toothache.
He sits next to me on the black leather couch and reaches his arm below, feeling around until he triumphantly pulls out Silvia's concealed tray with her secret stash of marijuana. "Bingo!" He looks at me and pushes his tattooed finger against his lip piercing. "Shhhh." When I realize I don't know anything about him other than he crashes here occasionally, he winks at me and starts rolling a joint.

"Where do you live?" I inquire. "Ah, now? I've been staying at the St. Mark's Hotel in downtown St. Petersburg. I'm doing tattoos over there, so it's alright for now." He comes to a halt and looks me in the eyes. "How old are you, anyway?" he says. "Eleven.", "Holy fuck! You're eleven? You've got to be kidding me." I flush and giggle. "What? Why?!"

Mikey, shaking his head in bewilderment, exclaims, "You look at least sixteen or seventeen.". I'm astounded. I've never been recognized in this way by a grown man. I think all my big garments couldn't hide what was going on underneath. "How old are you?" I inquire. He becomes solemn for a little moment. "Man, I'm twenty-six. It actually creeps up on you. You're a child one day and an adult the next..."

He reminds me of my father leaving me off on the first day of school and telling me it's all downhill from there. I'm not sure why these men are moaning about becoming older. They don't have expiration dates like women do. I pay attention to Mikey as he lights up the joint, takes a smoke, and passes it to me, but not without hesitation. "Should you even be smoking this? "Can I get in trouble for this?" I nudge him and grab the joint from his grasp, taking a hit and inhaling like a pro. I wash it down with a swallow of Jack Daniel's. "I'm an old soul, I guess." He glances into my eyes. "Yeah, I guess you are."

It's late, and most of the visitors have either gone home or are too messed up to move. I stand up to turn off the light. I can feel his eyes tracking my every motion across my body. Except for the glow from the TV screen, the room is pitch black. I feel his hand sliding closer to my leg as he throws a blanket over our legs. We both quiet down and pretend to watch the infomercial on TV, but the tension is palpable, and a tingling sensation passes through my body. "I know it might be wrong, but I don't give a fuck," he says abruptly to me. "I've been wanting to kiss you all night." My heart rate quickens. I've never done anything like this before. This isn't the same as kissing Ella. This feels mature. "Well, then, do it," I challenge him. He takes a little pause before his lips touch mine and I taste his tongue in my mouth. He smells like smoke and spearmint.

I let myself fall backward, bringing him down on top of me, and we continue to make out. I'm still a virgin. I'm not ready for sex. In addition, I didn't shave down there. When he gets up to use the restroom, I take advantage of the chance to sneak into Ella's room and hide on the top bunk. I'm only eleven years old, yet I recognize blue balls. I lie immobile in bed, my entire body covered by the covers. I can hear the toilet flushing. I expect him to come out and see me go. After a few moments, I noticed his silhouette at the doorway. I try not to make a sound by holding my breath. He stands there for a minute, peering into the darkness, before falling asleep on the couch. When I wake up the next morning, I'm relieved but also a little unhappy that he's gone.

After this thrilling experience, I begin to abandon my baggy clothes and accept my form. I'm addicted to the power I can wield over someone simply by being. I'm a B-cup, but the Victoria's Secret hot-pink padded bra I borrowed makes them appear like double D's. I got my mother's narrow waist, and my hips are getting bigger, just like hers. I also have the biggest butt, which the males at school constantly compliment. When he sees me in the corridor, one eighth-grade boy smacks it. This is apparently a compliment because it makes a lot of females in my grade envious, and I must confess that I enjoy the attention.

Silvia unexpectedly discloses that she has received a job offer in California and wants to relocate the entire family to Catalina Island. As I gulp down the knot developing in my throat, this startling announcement crushes me like a ton of bricks. "Why don't you just come with us?!" she asks. "You're practically family!" I'm not sure if she's intoxicated or serious, but I don't care since I'm overjoyed. I race home and search up this fabled spot called Catalina Island, and I immediately fall in love with what I see. Sun, beach, skin, and liberation! I even found a school on the beach that appears to be in paradise from the photographs I've seen online.

I quickly inform my father of my plans, and to my astonishment, he agrees to let me travel. He even calls Ella's mother to arrange the practicalities. I spend the following few days daydreaming about my future life in California with my sisters, but my joy is short-lived when my mother calls. I had forgotten about her. When I tell my mother about my plans to relocate, she responds with a stern "absolutely NO."

As I beg her, I can feel the wrath rising beneath the surface. "How can you have a say in my life when you don't even live here?!"As I anxiously try to reason with her, tears stream down the receiver. I explain the weather, the crime rate, and the family of sisters I would have, but she remains unconvinced. When questioned later, my father throws up his arms and says there's nothing he can do.

"Why can't you ever be a man and stand up to her?!" I yell at him. "You both ruined my fucking life!!!" I held onto them fiercely on the day of the relocation, refusing to let go. "Don't worry, sweetheart, you can come visit us whenever you want!" For the tenth time, Silvia reassures me. I nod, but I know deep down that I'll probably never see them again.

Ella contacts me a few times in the weeks following their relocation to Catalina, but I never hear from Silvia. My so-called family, I believe, moved on rather swiftly without me. Ella is likely to have a slew of girls competing to be her new closest friend. I tell myself that she doesn't need me. It's time for me to go.

In Ella's absence, I befriend Trisha, her other best friend. Trisha is stunning, although it's difficult to notice at first. Her beauty creeps up on you until you think she's the most gorgeous girl ever. Despite the fact that she lives across the street, Trisha rarely attends school. I used to be envious of her because Ella would spend the entire day with her and ignore me on the rare occasions that she did show up.

I'd watch them chuckle, as if they were part of an internal joke that only they knew about. I didn't get it. Trisha smells of rotten milk and cigarette smoke and wears the same dirty track trousers to school every day. Not to mention all the rumors I've heard about blow jobs in the park with older males.

She sits next to me during our knitting elective after school one day and begs to borrow one of my knitting needles. "I need to know about the blow jobs, is it true?" I blurted out after a little small conversation. She puts down her knitting and looks up at me. "Oh my goodness! Is that really still being discussed?!" She maintains her matter-of-fact tone, "It was the summer after fifth grade, and it was only one time with one guy, and he was my boyfriend that day."

"That day?!" Through my laughing, I inquired. "Well, I really wanted to try it but I didn't want to get called a slut, so I made him my boyfriend and dumped him right after." Her tone becomes more solemn. "And then he started spreading rumors about me." I nod. That makes sense. "How old was he?" I inquire.

"Seventeen." She sighs. I sigh. We go to the park after school, and she shows me exactly where the notorious blow job occurred, just in the bushes at the playground entrance. "It was nighttime, so there weren't any kids around," she assured me. We sat on her doorstep for a long time after escorting her home until I made the mistake of asking to use her bathroom. She pauses for a bit before saying, "Okay, but it's really messy, don't judge me."

I quickly reassure her that everything is fine. "My dad's a hoarder," I admit with a knowing grin. As we travel up the stairs in her building, I notice the foul odor intensifying with each step. It has a particular odor that is clearly hers. She unlocks the door and carefully opens it. A frightening heavy cloud of smoke bursts out into the hallway as she peers inside. The lights are turned out, and the blinds are shut, but the television casts a flickering glow over the mayhem. Once inside, I notice they live in a small studio apartment with two mattresses and a couch jammed into one room. My gaze darts around the floor, which is littered with periodicals, soiled clothes, and pill bottles. Every surface is littered with cigarette butts-filled cups and cans. The property appears to have not been cleaned in over a decade.

I'm taken aback when I see an elderly lady lying still on a bed, her limp body hooked up to a ventilator. Before I can grasp what I'm seeing, a raspy voice emerges from the shadows. I turn around to see Trisha's mother's frizzy hair peeking out from behind the television.
"Who the hell is this?" I told you not to bring any of your trashy pals here!" Something clicks, and I see a different side to Trish. "Oh, shut up, you drunken old cunt!" She needs to go to the potty!!!"

In Ella's absence, I befriend Trisha, her other best friend. Trisha is stunning, although it's difficult to notice at first. Her beauty creeps up on you until you think she's the most gorgeous girl ever. Despite the fact that she lives across the street, Trisha rarely attends school. I used to be envious of her because Ella would spend the entire day with her and ignore me on the rare occasions that she did show up. I'd watch them chuckle, as if they were part of an internal joke that only they knew about. I didn't get it. Trisha smells of rotten milk and cigarette smoke and wears the same dirty track trousers to school every day. Not to mention all the rumors I've heard about blow jobs in the park with older males.

She sits next to me during our knitting elective after school one day and begs to borrow one of my knitting needles. "I need to know about the blow jobs, is it true?" I blurted out after a little small conversation. She puts down her knitting and looks up at me. "Oh my goodness! Is that really still being discussed?!" She maintains her matter-of-fact tone, "It was the summer after fifth grade, and it was only one time with one guy, and he was my boyfriend that day."

"That day?!" Through my laughing, I inquired. "Well, I really wanted to try it but I didn't want to get called a slut, so I made him my boyfriend and dumped him right after." Her tone becomes more solemn. "And then he started spreading rumors about me." I nod. That makes sense. "How old was he?" I inquire. "Seventeen." She sighs. I sigh.

We go to the park after school, and she shows me exactly where the notorious blow job occurred, just in the bushes at the playground entrance. "It was nighttime, so there weren't any kids around," she assured me. We sat on her doorstep for a long time after escorting her home until I made the mistake of asking to use her bathroom. She pauses for a bit before saying, "Okay, but it's really messy, don't judge me."

I quickly reassure her that everything is fine. "My dad's a hoarder," I admit with a knowing grin. As we travel up the stairs in her building, I notice the foul odor intensifying with each step. It has a particular odor that is clearly hers. She unlocks the door and carefully opens it. A frightening heavy cloud of smoke bursts out into the hallway as she peers inside. The lights are turned out, and the blinds are shut, but the television casts a flickering glow over the mayhem. Once inside, I notice they live in a small studio apartment with two mattresses and a couch jammed into one room. My gaze darts around the floor, which is littered with periodicals, soiled clothes, and pill bottles. Every surface is littered with cigarette butts-filled cups and cans. The property appears to have not been cleaned in over a decade.

I'm taken aback when I see an elderly lady lying still on a bed, her limp body hooked up to a ventilator. Before I can grasp what I'm seeing, a raspy voice emerges from the shadows. I turn around to see Trisha's mother's frizzy hair peeking out from behind the television.

"Who the hell is this?" I told you not to bring any of your trashy pals here!" Something clicks, and I see a different side to Trish. "Oh, shut up, you drunken old cunt!" She needs to go to the potty!!!"

I start rinsing the dye out of her hair with the hose after what feels like thirty minutes. The water is extremely cold, and the only light on the dock is a reflection of the New Jersey skyline. "I can't fucking see anything!" I'm upset. When we rinse our hair, I notice that our clothes, fingers, feet, and faces are stained a deep red, and the dock now resembles the site of a gruesome murder. "We cannot go to school like this!" Trisha shouts.

I attempt scrubbing our clothes with the hose on the pier, but it doesn't work, so I propose we go grab some soap and lotion. I can tell she dislikes the concept. "Don't worry," I reassured, "we're in disguise now." The streets are dark and desolate after midnight. As we go back up the hill toward the CVS, we join arms. Trish suddenly squeezes my arm and motions to a lone police car sitting at the crossroads. When I see the two cops inside, a shiver runs down my spine.

"It's fine, they're just parked," I assure her. "Stop looking!"

We quicken our pace and begin crossing the street when the red and blue lights begin to flash, illuminating the entire block. Shit. We both keep our eyes forward as we scamper away, hoping they won't catch up with us. Then comes the dreaded "whoop-whoop." Trish takes my hand in hers and squeezes my fingers so hard that I can feel her heartbeat hammering through her palms. "Young ladies, stop walking.","Fuck," Trish exclaims. "Let me do the talking," I say quietly.

They stop in front of us and roll down their windows. "Mr. Officer, please allow us to explain. Her mother" He interrupts me. "I'm not interested in hearing it. "Get in your fucking car!", "But it's not safe for her to go"

They both exit their vehicle before I can finish my sentence and grab us by the back of the head, pushing us into the automobile by our hair. On my way in, I hit my head against the door. "Fucking pigs!" Trish cries in the back seat, and I yell. I try to console her, knowing it's all my fault. I, too, begin to cry. "I apologize. I'm truly sorry, Trish. I'm very sorry."

Trisha is the first to be dropped off. When we arrive, her mother is already waiting for her outside, dressed in a soiled big men's T-shirt and flip-flops. She had a large Band-Aid on her brow, a cigarette and cup in one hand, and a house phone in the other. As the police unlock the car door, Trisha and I scramble into the backseat, clutching each other for dear life. "Don't worry, I'm gonna come save you!" I scream as the officers pull us apart and drag her back into the custody of her mother. Her mother snatches her arm and pulls her inside, turning around to shout at me, "Stay away from my daughter!!"

We arrived at my residence a few minutes later. My father is taken aback to see me being escorted by police officials, owing to the fact that he had no idea I was absent. "What the hell did you do to your hair?" asked the man. I just roll my eyes and go to the bathroom.

"Hmm... I'm not sure... "Perhaps you need a different size," she suggests. The sales worker rushes to buy me the same thing in two sizes, while I grab my other clothes from the rack and toss the hangers in another room. Finally, they've lost track of how many items I have in my fitting room. We take out the plastic alarm sensors, leaving little holes in the cloth, and walk out, waving to the personnel. Simply behave normally.

I'm hooked on the rush, that unexplainable sensation that washes over my entire body. My heart rate increases, my steps become lighter, and my stomach flutters. I leave the store with two Ed Hardy T-shirts and a pair of True Religions under my Juicy Couture sweatpants. Score! Nothing compares the excitement of walking past metal detectors and getting away with it in my new jeans.

We take the train downtown, frequently squeezing in between cars for a quick hurry. We hang out in Union Square and in Astor Place's Cube. We travel to Saint Mark's and flirt with an old tattoo artist who offers everyone of us a free tattoo. Trisha gets a tramp stamp and I get a cartoon cat dangling from a rose in the exact location as my mom had a tattoo. Our nipples are pierced. We're only twelve, but my father claims we're worse than the girls in the movie Thirteen. He chuckles and finds it amusing.

My father enters my room one day with a solemn expression on his face. "Look, girls, I have to tell you something for your own benefit... Do not inhale the PCP angel dust. It causes brain hair to develop. Weed, heroin, cocaine... All of that nonsense is good. But keep that angel dust away from me!"
Trisha and I burst out laughing when he left.

When I return home from school one winter day, I notice the answering machine's light blinking. I push the play button and hear Trisha's shaky and panicked voice shouting into the receiver. Through the sobs, I can hardly understand what she's saying. "She's taking me, Julia!" She's going to take me to Oklahoma! "I don't want to go!" In the background, I can hear her mother shouting incoherently. "Shut the fuck up, Mom!" I don't want to say good-bye!"

I'm completely taken aback. I take up the phone and try to contact her back, but there is no answer. They've already left; it's too late. It was over in an instant. I didn't think much of Trisha's absence from school that day. I despise myself for failing to save her.

I felt like a zombie for the next few days. I'm unable to eat or sleep. I go to school and then come home to wait by the phone. I replay her upsetting message over and over. I inquired about the driving time to Oklahoma with Jeeves. In bed, I listen to Coldplay while using the hair dryer to conceal my sobbing. "Why does everyone always leave me?" I scream into my pillow. "It's not fair!!!"

Two weeks later, the call arrives. When the phone rings and I see an Oklahoma area code, I'm overjoyed. I raise the receiver and exclaim, "What took you so long?!"

"We just got a phone finally!" Trish states. "Please tell me everything!" "I've been concerned about you."

"It's not so horrible after all. It's always hot here, and our trailer is quite large."

"Have you made any friends?" I inquired about her. "Yeah, I hung out with the neighbors, and didn't tell anyone but I smoked crystal meth!"

"Whoa, that sounds so cool!" With a hint of envy in my voice, I say.
"It was, but I don't think I'm gonna do it again." I muster the confidence to ask the dreaded question: "Are you ever coming back?"

"My mother lost her flat. She claims she needs some time to get back on her feet, but who knows?"

Trisha appears unconcerned with my situation. I determine right then and there that I, too, must move on. If she can make new acquaintances, I can, too. This is where Rose enters the picture. Rose attends some of my lessons and is very different from Trisha. She is unlike anyone else. I'm certain she's an angel. She speaks softly. She is reserved. She is unadulterated. She's also wealthy. Rich Fifth Avenue penthouse. I enjoy breaking into her home after her mother has gone to bed. We sit cross-legged on her floor, facing each other, and exchange love poems. I put her name on my sneakers, and she puts mine on hers. We occasionally massage each other with oils. We occasionally dribble hot wax on each other's bodies. We occasionally take baths together, and I can't help but notice her big double-D breasts, which are covered in thick purple stretch marks.

Our school's lads don't really like her that way, but I think she's the most gorgeous girl in the world. When I make her giggle, tears rush down her charmingly freckled cheeks until she pees her pants. Her skin is white and as smooth as snow. Her arms, in particular, are my favorite. She always smells like a drugstore vanilla body mist, which I find enticing. I even know how long it takes me to go from my place to hers. Seven. "You're my soulmate," I say. "No, you're MY soulmate," she responds. Our bond is so strong that all of her friends refer to us as lesbians. Rose is friends with the popular females, all of whom regard Rose to be their best friend. That may be true, but she assures me that I am hers. When the popular girls learn that I always have a stale pack of cigarettes from Italy in my backpack, they welcome me into their group. I don't even smoke them; I simply like feeling like an adult.

Dominique is someone I've known since elementary school. She currently resides in Brooklyn. We used to have sleepovers at each other's houses all the time, and she once told me I was her best friend. She wasn't, however, mine. We clashed frequently because she envied my bond with Danny. The fights were largely about her tormenting me and convincing everyone else to exclude me. She started crying after I fought back one day, and she never bothered with me again.

Abeline was chosen the most attractive girl in school. She's Dominican and from the Bronx. She enjoys singing and dancing, and many of the males like her, including Tommy, my crush. Tara is a Jewish woman who lives on Manhattan's Upper East Side. She has her hair straightened chemically and never wears the same clothing twice. She lives with her mother, a successful attorney who had her at a late age, and they have a fluffy little white puppy who barks a lot.

We call ourselves the Stoned Monroes, and we quickly start bringing out the worst in one another. If the females in the lower grades are prettier than us, we bully them. We released mice in the school. We scare teachers so much that they cry. We sprayed "Stoned Monroes" all over the corridors. We unbolted the doors from their hinges. We are suspended because we fought.

My grades are failing, and my personal life is a living nightmare. My mother is now pregnant, and I overhear my parents talking about the baby's due date, with my mother assuring my father that he is the father. I'm just astonished they're still having sex because they appear to dislike each other. My mother wishes to give birth in New York and take maternity leave, so she will be present at all times. I'm not used to being that close to her, and it's safe to say that it's not working out. She invades my space, infringes on my freedom, violates my independence, enters my room, and throws out whatever she doesn't like. We have heated arguments in which I shout, "I hate you!!" to which she coldly answers, "I hate you even more." There is no attempt to conceal our mutual hatred. I even sleep with my luggage packed, ready to flee if things become too dangerous.

The cops have already arrived several times. She whipped me with computer wires once when she was six months pregnant in front of two officers who did nothing. In the distance, I heard my father say, "You can't do that in America, sweetheart." As if she doesn't realize. As if they didn't always defeat us. As if he ever refers to her as sweetheart.

I flee. I seek sanctuary in Rose's friendly house whenever possible. When that isn't an option, I make do with whatever shelter I can find, which can range from unlocked cars to 24-hour delis, roofs, and park benches. Anywhere is preferable to staying at home. I ran to the hospital to be by my mother's side when she went into delivery. A nurse suggests an epidural while she is breathing through contractions. But before my mother can respond, my father weighs in: "No, she wants to have a natural birth." My father is met with a look of disgust from the nurse. "I wasn't questioning you, sir. I'll ask you when you're in labor." It's so satisfying to hear her tell him to fuck off quietly. My mother also tells him to quiet up.

Finally, my baby brother is born, and I am overcome with emotion as I hold him in my arms. But the moment is ruined when my father hits me across the face for not wearing gloves.

Instead of being pleased on my trip home, I am bitter. That was wrecked for me by him. I exact my vengeance by creeping into his bed at night and snatching cash from his wallet. The more harm he causes, the more money I collect. The next day at school, a girl in my class tells me loudly that her aunt was the nurse at the hospital who delivered my little brother, and that my father was a horrible jerk. I'm humiliated. Creative writing is the only subject in which I thrive. Or, at least, I used to excel at it until becoming involved with the wrong crew. Ms. Williams, my instructor, approaches me after class one afternoon and expresses her concern. "You used to be one of my more promising students," she said. "But now I'm not so sure, and I'm afraid…"

I know she's correct, so I don't argue with her. She's already jokingly referred to me as the "queen of excuses."

"I hate to see wasted talent," she cautions, her lips pursed and her eyes welling up with tears. "Have you considered what you want to be when you grow up?" Will you attend college? Because I'm warning you that if you continue on your current path, no reputable high schools or institutions will take you." I nod. "I know. All I want to do is get through the day. "Right now, I can't think that far ahead." She takes a breather. "Write about it," she says before dismissing me. I'm annoyed that I care what Ms. Williams thinks of me. Normally, I couldn't care less what other people thought of me. But the prospect of disappointing her makes me nervous. I'm curious whether this is how most people feel when they fail their parents.

After school, I go to my bathroom alone and let the ink pour across the sheet, releasing the sorrow and emotions I'd repressed deep inside. Each stroke of my pen feels like a weight being lifted from my shoulders. I write about the suffocating sense of insignificance and the never-ending struggle to find my place in the world. I write about how lonely I am and how everyone always abandons me, which causes me to put on a strong and aggressive face. I write about the want to compare myself to others and the feelings of inadequacy that arise. I fantasize about what my life would have been like if I had been born into a regular, loving family, and how I would be different.

The following day, I nervously handed my work to Ms. Williams at the start of class. Later that day, she approaches me privately and asks if she can read it for the class as an anonymous contribution. "No one will know you wrote it," she promises. "I was moved by your writing, Julia." She insists that my work can serve as an example to my classmates. I'm wondering whether she's going to ask if I'm all right. I'm scared about sharing something so intimate with what feels like the entire globe. But I give in and give her my permission.

Ms. Williams reads my writing aloud to the class the next day. My palms begin to sweat as I hear her recount my agony. Even when I hear it in her voice, my tragedy feels horrifyingly familiar. Some of my students snicker and make deliberate noises, which makes me feel foolish and insignificant. "Corny," someone says, and I know who wrote it even though they don't. That's enough to make me feel degraded. Ms. Williams does not inquire as to my well-being. From then on, I vowed to keep everything inside and never again expose my vulnerability with anyone.

Chapter 3:
MOTHERLAND

When we arrive in Italy, my mother drives us four hours north to the small mountain cottage that has been in our family for generations. It's not the most gorgeous house in the world, but it's survived two wars and served as the setting for some of my favorite childhood memories. My mother would frequently leave Chris and me with our grandfather in June and fetch us up in September.

Grandpa used to pour buckets of cold water on the boys who came roaring at our window at night when we were kids. We captured spiders and scaled walls in order to gather wild strawberries from a nearby garden. We made firewood aircraft and drank water straight from the cascade. The town is quite small. Everyone is related in some way, and everyone is aware of one other's activities. Growing up, the locals treated me as if I were a celebrity simply because I lived in New York. They'd exclaim, "Americana!" And stop to take photos with me, explaining how we were linked and telling me stories of my mother when she was a tiny child.

We are met by our neighbors and family friends, who all comment on how long it has been and how different I look. I'm not sure if that's a complement or not. I set my belongings down, dress into my cutest outfit, and dash down the road to my cousin Chiara's place. She's a year my senior and the most amusing person I know. We met in town as youngsters and later discovered that, surprise, surprise, we were connected. Chiara is a chimney-smoker who drinks like a sailor and curses like a truck driver. Her father also strikes her frequently. I once stepped between them and was chased around the house with a wooden paddle. He does, however, create the finest paninis. We always return to their house for lunch because she spends every night sleeping in our attic bedroom.

The local bartenders have no trouble providing us drinks or selling us cigarettes. Chiara doesn't wear as much makeup as I do, and she never wears thongs or padded bras like I do. "You're such a show-off," she remarks as I get ready for a night out. "I'm an American now," I say boldly. She dismisses me with a roll of the eyes. "Italian women are raised to be modest and blend in."

I remove my mascara and make direct eye contact with her through the mirror. Chiara pauses to consider my words and looks at herself in the mirror. Her eyeliner becomes bolder with time, and she begins to borrow my collection of slinky tank tops and low-rise trousers. We skip down the mountain together and to the bar, where we take shots of vodka back-to-back until we can't move. I like to flirt with gorgeous older men who ride motorbikes and drive muscle vehicles.

The younger boys in town don't pique my interest in the same way. It gives me such a high when I master the art of seduction. When they find out I'm just fourteen, most of them don't care.

Chiara is irritated by my shenanigans. "I'm not sure why you need everyone to like you. It gives the impression that you are desperate and insecure."
"You're just jealous 'cause they like me more than you!"

"Of course they like you more, you have your tits in their face all night!"

I push her, she slaps me, I slap her back, and we're grappling in the dirt in no time. When I hear someone remark, "Girls, come on, you're too pretty for this!" I had her pinned to the ground, sitting on her chest and giggling. I raise my head and meet the most beautiful man I've ever seen. I quickly get off of her and rearrange my clothes, but he's already gone.

I'm playing UNO with Chiara and a local youngster the next day when the mystery man walks by again. "Girls," he adds, winking and nodding, but he's only staring at me. My heart is hammering in my cheeks. I return his smile and nod, my gaze following him all the way to his car, a purple Porsche Cayenne. He glides into his vehicle with ease, each movement seamlessly transitioning into the next. I've never seen a man so graceful. He restarts his car and returns to our direction, pausing as he passes us again. He steals another glimpse, and our gazes connect for a fraction of a second, but it's as if lightning struck.

A few weeks pass with no further sightings of the mysterious stranger. I lose interest until one night, while we're sitting on a bench on our cobblestone street talking with a neighbor, I notice him driving by. He turns on his headlights, parks his car, and exits. He is holding a bottle of Anima Nera, which translates to "Black Soul" in Italian. It's a thick, silky liqueur with anise and licorice notes. "I'm Giovanni, what's your name?" he asks the neighbor, ignores Chiara, and introduces himself to me. I can't get enough of his deep Venetian drawl. I notice his beautiful eyelashes and his scent, which is lovely and almost feminine. "Julia," I mumble. "And this is my cousin Chiara.", "Hi, Chiara, nice to meet you," he replies before returning his gaze to me. "I hate to break up this little lovefest, but I'd like a drink," Chiara says, utterly unaware of how embarrassing she is. He laughs and hands her the Anima Nera bottle. She takes a large swallow and then hands it to me. I take a swig, then another, and another till I can't stand straight any longer.

Chiara leaves with the neighbor, leaving Giovanni and myself alone. We're sitting next to each other under a tiny bridge, talking about life. He's doing most of the talking as I try to hide my inebriation. He tells me he's twenty-three years old and has lived in this town his entire life. He is looking forward to bringing his children here one day. He tells me about his employment and how he works in Venice for his father's company. He claims his father is a jerk and his mother is controlling, bugging him about getting married and settling down. As the world around me warps and my mind whirl in circles beneath my eyelids, I nod. I nod as he walks away, doing my best to maintain my cool and appear mature.

"I can't believe I didn't meet you sooner," he says softly as he leans in and kisses my lips. My eyes are still closed as he rises up abruptly. "I'm gonna get another bottle out of my car." I stumble behind him, attempting to walk in a straight line. He rummages about in his trunk until he finds a bottle of red wine. He cracks it open and takes a sip before handing it to me. I take a sip and pass it back. We stand awkwardly, giggling, beneath the moon and millions of stars that light up the sky above us. "You have beautiful eyelashes," I say.

He leans in for another kiss. He scoops me up this time, and I straddle him in the middle of the cobblestone road. We collapse on the ground, tongues wagging, laughing and kissing. He takes my bra off and pushes my shirt up, kissing my breasts. For a little moment, I undo his pants and admire his penis. He is not circumcised. It's not the largest, but it's lovely. I suck it for a few seconds before deciding that tonight is the night. I squat over him and sit on it, pulling my pants down. This is not at all sexy, and it feels unpleasant and unnatural.

It doesn't go in right away. He thrusts harder and harder until something snaps deep within my gut. When I see his magnificent penis coated in blood, my eyes widen and I'm brought back to reality. Droplets of blood trickle down my legs and land all over his Polo cable-knit sweater with the American flag on it, and I get up. He looks stunned for a time, then irritated because I've destroyed his sweater.

"You didn't tell me you were a virgin," he said. "You didn't ask," I point out. "I'd better get you home," he adds quietly as he walks me back toward my house. We say our goodbyes with an awkward peck on the cheek. I sprint up the stairs and peer out my bathroom window to see him walk home. He removes his sweater and examines it briefly before dumping it into his trunk. When he walks into his house, I rush into the bathtub and begin scrubbing my skin vigorously when I hear a car pull up. When I look out the window, I see the neighbor hauling Chiara's limp corpse out of his back seat, which is fully coated in vomit.

I race to her aid and help her up the three flights of stairs. I drew her a bath and rinsed the vomit pieces out of her hair, hoping she wasn't incoherent so I could tell her about how I just lost my virginity. I really wish I could call Rose. I wish I could speak with someone.

I snuggle Chiara into bed and dash down to the cellar, where I mount on my bike and pedal into the morning as fast as I can. As I ride through the clouds, soaring up the mountain, I feel the morning dew on my skin. I arrive at a small lonely stone church, drop my bike, kneel, and seek forgiveness. It begins to pour as tears stream down my cheeks. I tell myself that no amount of water can ever wipe away the filth and embarrassment I feel.

Before I can even absorb what happened the next day, news travels throughout town that I'm a whore. My friend's aunt awoke in the middle of the night after hearing us outside. She noticed us doing it and cracked open the window. She even told Giovanni's mother, who now believes I'm a whore as well. "I overheard the clerk calling you a lowlife whore at the store today," she tells me. I sigh. Except for Giovanni, I don't care what others think of me.

He slows his automobile in front of my house late at night and beams his headlights, signaling me to come down. We converse in his car and sometimes make out. But generally, he criticizes me for having calloused hands, biting my nails, or not properly brushing my hair. He sighs and shakes his head: "You're just a kid." I despise the fact that he doesn't take me seriously.

During the day, I walk up the mountain alone and lie in the dirt. I deal with God, cursing Him while appealing with Him. "Oh, God, please make Giovanni fall in love with me." I promise I'll do my best. I'm going to quit smoking and stop stealing money from my father or grandfather."

Giovanni has taken over my head, and he understands how much power he has over me. He has me under his grip with crumbs, and I beg him to let me free. He says okay, but he always returns. We are trapped on this loop for the rest of the summer until I notice him packing suitcases into his trunk down the street one morning while sitting on my rooftop. I rush downstairs barefoot and hurry to the end of my short driveway to wait for him, pretending to be there by chance. He slows down as he passes my house, like he always does, and we lock eyes. He nods, and I nod, as if we've reached an unspoken understanding. He presses the accelerator, and I watch as his automobile fades into a tiny purple speck in the distance. I want to chase after him or yell at him to stop, but I know I can't.

I can't wait to pick up Rose after school when I return to New York. As kids rush out of the building, I eagerly stand outside. After what seems like an eternity of waiting, I begin to worry that I may have missed her. Kids hug, link arms, and rush away until I'm the only one left. I stand alone, awkwardly biting my nails, until I see her emerge with a bunch of girls. She's already made a lot of new pals, as I predicted. She notices me and hastily waves goodbye as I jump across the street and embrace her, scooping her up and spinning her in circles. "I love you, I love you, I love you," I repeat, snuggled in her neck. I take a deep breath in. She's wearing JLo's perfume.

I start telling her about Italy, Giovanni, late-night motorbike excursions, and how simple it is to buy cigarettes. But she appears to be preoccupied as she taps away on her Nokia. "How was your first day?!" I inquire, excitedly. "It was okay." She keeps tapping. "How about you?" "That's not good. This morning, they confiscated my pipe at the metal detectors and said " She interrupts me. "Should we go meet everyone at John Jay?"

I shrug and nod, remembering Rose's disinterest in spending time with anyone but me. I'm not impressed when we get to the park. I'm not sure what it is, but I feel different. It's as if I aged ten years in one summer, and everything I used to enjoy no longer does. Everyone else, on the other hand, appears to be the same. Childish. They swarm around me as I tell them about my wild adventures in Italy. When I tell them I had sex behind a church, they all gasp. After a while, everyone disperses, and I become bored. When I find Rose and tell her I'm leaving, she seems perplexed and almost insulted. I can sense she wants to remain, so I don't invite her, and for the first time in my life, I leave early.

I find myself thinking about Italy for the next few days. I'm missing my grandfather and my buddies. I miss being able to stroll into a bar and get a drink, and I miss Giovanni in particular. I'm suffocating in my house, surrounded by my mother and the baby. I decided to return to Italy and approach my mother with the proposal. "If you let me move to Italy, I'll be out of your hair."

She loves the idea, and a few weeks later, I'm saying goodbye to my friends and flying back to Italy with her. She enrolls me in the same Catholic school where she was educated as a child. She meets with the head priest, who tells us that he has found a family willing to host me for a few months. I'm frustrated and wish I could just live alone or an hour away with my grandfather, who was recently diagnosed with prostate cancer. My mother said, "He needs to get through his chemo and with the way you behave, you'll send him to his grave early." It's becoming clear to me that the reality of my circumstance does not correspond to my fantasies. I didn't agree to live with a group of strangers.

My mother reminds me to be careful on the way to my new surrogate family's place. As we drive in circles through the dreary tiny town on the outskirts of Como, it begins to rain. We arrive at the house and pull into the driveway. I pucker my brow in disgust at the large dismal gray home in front of us. "I'm not going to be able to live here!" This place is terrifying!" My mother whips around and smothers me. "It's either this or homelessness!" As my mother rings the doorbell, I roll my eyes and stare out into the haze. She notices her reflection in the mirror and begins to fix her hair. A young lady with a short pixie cut welcomes us with a tight-lipped smile as the door swings wide. As she takes us inside, my gaze darts across the room, taking in everything. The room is clean and cool. There is nothing out of place. In a tracksuit and slippers, a tall, slender middle-aged woman with short hair enters from the kitchen and welcomes us in. "You must be Julia!" she exclaimed excitedly in shaky English. "We are happy to meet you."

When I respond to her in Italian, her smile fades to a scowl. "Oh, what a shame, I was hoping we could all brush up on our English while you were here!" She chuckles. I gave my mother a look. "My name is Rossana, this is my daughter, Letizia, and you'll meet my husband, Paolo, later." Most nights, he comes home late." She walks us around their house and tells us where I'll be staying, which is a modest guest room with terra-cotta tiles and a twin bed. I notice a desk with a computer on the other side of the room. Score! I'll wait till everyone is asleep before connecting to AIM.

My mother conducts most of the talking as I pick at my meal at supper. I try to ask Letizia questions and get one-word responses. I begin to worry if she despises me. As dessert is served, I begin to dread the moment my mother must depart. I'm back to feeling like a kid. She brings me a small Nokia after supper. "There are fifty euros on this. Don't spend it all at once, since I'm not going to give you any more."

I accompany her to her car, where we hug and she reminds me once more to behave. Her headlights fade into the distance as I watch. I smoke a cigarette once she's gone and the coast is clear, but I only get a few puffs before I'm called back inside. "I think I'll go unpack," I say to Rossana. "I'll help you!" she declares emphatically.

As I take my items from my luggage, I notice her critical eyes inspecting everything. I fold my things and put them in the closet, and she takes them out and refolds them right away.

"So, why did you want to leave New York?!" she exclaims, stunned. I don't tell her about the fighting, Giovanni, or my grandfather's illness. "I just prefer Italy." "Best country in the world," I say, forcing a smile. "Brava!" She gives me a pat on the back.

When she eventually departs, I rush to the computer and push the power button, only to be greeted by a password prompt. Fuck! I pull out my phone and dial Rose's number, but every time I reach her voicemail, money is removed from my phone card. I'm tempted to text Giovanni, but I promised myself I'd never contact him again. I even erased his phone number from my phone. I do, however, have his phone number memorized. The simple prospect of hearing his voice energises my soul and sends a surge of adrenaline coursing through my body. I retype my message several times before eventually summoning the guts to press the submit button.

"Hi G. It's Julia calling. I am currently residing in Italy. We should meet up if you're ever in Como." I reread my message till it begins to seem ridiculous. I'm humiliated. I lie in bed, my gaze drawn to the lights of passing cars dancing on the ceiling. My ideas echo in my head, only heightened by the silence that surrounds me. Hours pass in silence as I wonder, "What the fuck did I get myself into?"

When Rossana walks into my room, it's still dark outside. She summons me to the kitchen, where Letizia is already seated, sipping a coffee and munching on a croissant.

"Buongiorno," I greet with the warmest smile I can muster. "Ciao," she says without looking up.

Rossana pushes us out of the house after breakfast and takes us to a remote rail station in the dark. I light a cigarette on the platform and watch the sunrise in the frigid cold after she's gone. When Letizia gets in my face, I realize how bad this is. "My mother is aware that you smoke. She discovered a cigarette butt on the grass. She told you you couldn't do it anymore." I take a deep breath and blow it at her. I'm laughing. She isn't. She coughs, and when the train arrives, she takes the seat farthest away from me.

We're off to a fantastic start. To make matters worse, Giovanni never responded to me. Letizia exits at the final stop, and I follow her. I walk a few yards behind her, keeping a close eye on her because I'm not sure where I'm heading. As we get closer to the school, I notice swarms of kids spread in various cafés, sipping espressos and puffing on cigarettes. We come across a large sign that says "Internet Café." I look inside, where smoke is rising from a dark staircase leading down to a basement. I take a breather and return my gaze to Letizia. I say fuck it and turn sharply to dash down into the basement.

When I get downstairs, the familiar sound of Amerie's "One Thing" playing on MTV from a small TV on the wall greets me. The music is blaring, and the children are even louder. I dash to the rows of machines and log on to AOL. When I check in, I see that Trisha is the only one who is online. "Trish!!" I start typing rapidly. You won't believe I moved to Italy..." I notice her typing. I keep an eye on the time as I wait for her response. The typing comes to a halt. I then say, "I miss you." I took a peek at the time. I'm already running late for class. Finally, a message comes, saying, "I know! Rose informed me! I relocated from Oklahoma to New York City. I now live in Harlem with my father. I'm sorry you're not here:("I'm feeling nauseous. Trisha has returned to town, and she's hanging out with Rose while I'm not there! I try to be happy for them, but a part of me wonders how their lives carried on without me.

"Do you communicate with Rose?" I've been attempting to contact her.", "Ya. I'll see her tomorrow. She does have a boyfriend. Ace. You can look him up. He's in her MySpace top eight.", "Wtf is MySpace?"

As I wait for her response, I receive notification that she has logged off. When I take my gaze away from the computer, I notice that the café is deserted and that everyone has gone to class. I ask the clerk for instructions, and he directs me to my school. I rush through the plaza, pumped up on adrenaline and nervous energy.

When I arrive late for class, Letizia raises an eyebrow before muttering something to her seatmate. The lecturer interrupts his lecture to ask me my name. "I'm Julia Fox."

Across the room, I hear a few snickers. "Oohh, the American girl!"
I nod, and he motions to an open desk. When the lecturer asks me to answer a question, I take out my books and start sketching and daydreaming. "Can you please repeat the question?" I ask. "Who can help out Miss Fox?" Letizia raises her hand and asks, sarcastically, "What's the difference between an adverb and an adjective?"

My face is starting to burn. The temperature in the room has suddenly increased by ten degrees. This is something I should know. I am aware of the answer. I'm aware of it. My favorite subject is creative writing. But I'm too scared. I go blank. "I… I'm afraid I don't know." Around the room, gasps are harmonizing like a lousy chorus.

Grammar was never taught to me. I never studied anatomy or art history. I knew nothing about Greece or the Roman Empire. Christopher Columbus discovered America, I learned. I'm overwhelmed by the number of classes I'm required to take, including Latin, German, geometry, and calculus. And each professor assigns hours of homework per night, making it hard to stroll through as I used to. To make matters worse, school is held on Saturdays.

As soon as school is out, I phone my mother and ask her to let me come home. "Not at all, Julia. You wanted to do it, and now you have to finish it." She cuts me off. When I phone my father, he says, "Absolutely fucking not." We paid a lot of money for you to attend this school!" He also hangs up on me. I contact them often and send them a barrage of text messages till my phone credit runs out. Letizia informs me on the train journey home that the two girls who sit behind me in class are keeping track of the color of my thongs in their notebook.

When we reach home, Rossana leads us into the dining room to begin the four hours of studying for the next day. My head shakes. Isn't this woman living her life? She sets a dish of snacks on the table and says, "When you're finished, you can both use the computer for a half hour." I'm relieved because now I have something to look forward to. We do our schoolwork after a few endless hours at the table. Rossana examines it and, once satisfied, excuses us from the table.

Letizia dashes into my room, leaving me in her wake. She sits down at her desk and cries out to her mother. After a few minutes, her mother walks in and tells us to close our eyes. I attempt peeping at the keyboard as she types the password, but I can't tell what she's entering. Letizia puts on a computer game and begins playing it in silence after she departs.

After a few minutes, I summoned the guts to ask, "Can I please use the computer when you're done?" Her gaze is fixated on the television. "Yeah, when I'm done." I'm sitting on my bed, going over my texts with my folks again. "Okay, girls, thirty minutes is up," Rossana says as she knocks on the door. I'm going to turn off the computer. It's time to go to bed."

"But I still haven't had the chance to use it!" I jump out of bed and tell her. Rossana casts a glance at Letizia, who responds, "I lost track of time!" Rossana sighs and shakes her head. "If you can't share, I'm taking away computer privileges!"

Letizia groans as her mother approaches from behind her and smushes the power button with her long bony finger. "I didn't even save the game!" Letizia smashes her hands on the desk and flees the room. Rossana follows her, scolding her. I freaking despise it here.

I take the train eagerly the next morning, ignoring Letizia and peering out the window at the ever-changing landscapes speeding by. I'm the first to get off the train when we reach the station, heading directly for the Internet café. I enter "MySpace" into the search engine and press the enter key. I'm taken to a website where I'm asked to create an account and log in. I start typing my pals' names into the search field one by one. I finally locate Rose's profile and check her Top 8, and there he is: Ace.

When I go on his profile, I'm astounded to learn that he has over 10,000 pals. I tell myself that he can't possibly have that many pals. I navigate through his photo album by clicking on his default photo. What I saw astounds me: stacks of cash, a scale next to a mountain of cocaine on a glass table, and so many guns. I wonder what he's doing with Rose as I conceal the computer screen from any prospective spectators. Is their relationship serious? What do they discuss? Is she getting high with him? I'm overcome with worry.

I open AIM and write Trish once again: "I don't have any more minutes on my phone." Could you kindly instruct Rose to contact me?" I have to leave for class before she can respond. I spent the entire day expecting Rose to phone or text. I still write poems in my notebook for her. So I don't forget anything, I write her extensive letters of what I'll say to her when I eventually get the chance to speak with her.

Letizia and I rush home after school to finish our homework in silence, and when it's computer time, I rush to the room first and wait for Rossana to input the password. Letizia sits on the edge of the desk, watching me surf the web. "What is Myspace?" she inquires. I can tell she's enthralled with the cast of characters on the TV. "Do you know these people?"

I open AIM and, by some miracle, Rose is online. "Rosie! Please contact me. I texted you using my Italian phone number. I absolutely need to speak with you!" My phone begins to vibrate a few moments later. It is her. I grab my phone and dash into the bathroom. "Rosie! I really miss you. I'm very depressed. Moving here was a terrible mistake for me. It irritates me. They make us do so much work and force us to attend school on weekends... High school lasts five years! Not four, as in the United States. "Are you there, Rosie?"

"Uh-huh," she admits. "Are you mad at me?" I inquired about her. She takes a breather. "No! I could never be angry with you. I'm just too busy "I interrupted her. "I noticed you have a boyfriend!" He's adorable. "How did you first meet him?" "Ace?! He is not my lover. We're only getting started.", "Don't lie to me!", "I'm not!", "Do you like him?", "I suppose. To be honest, I'm sick of everybody asking me about him."Ouch. "Okay, well, I just wanted to check in, you feel so far away.", "I am far away.", "That's not what I mean.", "You've gone, Julia. I'm at a loss for words. I have to live my life as well."

The talk stalls between awkward silences. "My mom's calling me, can I call you back?" she says. "Of course, yeah." I adore you. "Please contact me again!" She hangs up, and I know she's not going to call me back. I strip quietly, turn on the hot water, curl up in a ball on the shower floor, and cry. A knock at the door startles me after a few minutes.

"Don't use up all the hot water!" Rossana yells from behind the closed door. "It's almost time for bed!", "Okay!" I exclaim after swallowing some water. I recline on the floor, resting my head on my knees. I freaking despise it here.

The next morning, I'm relieved to find that classes have been canceled due to "Culture Day," in which each classroom is transformed into a different country. I'm walking aimlessly through the halls when I come across "Spain" and discover a large bowl of sangria left untouched on a desk. I make a beeline for the bowl and order two double-fist glasses of sangria. I'm slumped over the toilet, puking my brains out before I realize it. I hear a bunch of young women enter the restroom. "Wait, is somebody puking in here?" one of them exclaims. I open the stall and apologize, "I guess I drank too much sangria." The females burst out laughing and patted my back. "Are you kidding me?" says the girl with long ashy-blonde hair. I absolutely adore this girl! "Please get her some water." The brunette girl dashes out of the restroom to get it. "I'm Barbara." She extends her hand before retracting it. "You know what, why don't you wash your hands first." Every word she says is met with belly laughter. The brunette girl returns with a cup of water, which I guzzle down and thank them for.

"Where did you come from?" Barbara inquires. "I'm from New York."

"Oh, you're the girl from New York!" We've heard good things about you! Seriously, what the fuck are you doing here? "Are you insane?!" I'm being bombarded with inquiries from all sides when one of them says, "We're going to the café." "Would you like to join us?" I nod and smile.

They take me to the same basement café I've been to before. At first, my gaze is drawn to the computers, and I have to battle the impulse to go online. Barbara shoots question after question at me. They are captivated as I tell them about my life in New York. They freak out when I show them my nipple ring. They're all in a grade higher than mine. Barbara is the most amusing of the group. Tatiana is the most beautiful, and Sara is the sweetest. I discovered that they are all in long-term partnerships. Sara has been in a relationship with her boyfriend since middle school. Barbara is also engaged and has a ring on her finger. She's known him since she was eleven years old. He is older than she is, but her family adores him and supports their marriage preparations. Tatiana enjoys fucking married men in her little town. She's been secretly dating the butcher for the past two years. This discovery has taken me by surprise. People in America move through relationships like toilet paper, and childhood lasts far beyond our forties. I can't believe how knowledgeable these girls are. They wear heels to class every day. They always have flawlessly coiffed highlighted hair and wear layers of bronzer. The only thing we have in common is that we all smoke cigarettes in a chain, but not in a rebellious manner. They do it in a stylish manner. In my Nirvana T-shirts and shredded skinny jeans, I look considerably younger than they do.

When it's time to leave, they all make a point of getting my phone number. We exchange kisses on the cheek and agree to meet in the café the next morning. I skip to the station, feeling a gleam of hope for the first time in a long time. On weekends, I go to see my grandfather instead of spending time with my host family. I enjoy the coziness of our Saronno flat, where we can sit around and watch TV all day. He still has his booze and cigarettes, but this time I have them as well. I look after stuff around the house. I assist him in bathing, administering his chemo doses, and preparing his meals.

I wait until he's asleep before going through the cabinets, unearthing all the mementos we left behind when we moved. I dig through my mother's drawers, trying on her old things in front of the mirror. I discover an extra set of keys to her unoccupied Como apartment. I removed the landline to connect to the Internet on my laptop and speak with my friends in New York all night. When Grandpa finds me on the computer, he exclaims, "You're going to bankrupt me!!!" I sigh and roll my eyes. How much can it actually cost?

I log on one night and Trish immediately messages me. "Rose was taken to rehab!!! Her sister said that two men kidnapped her in the middle of the night and that their mother paid them to do so!! Since then, no one has heard from her!" I go to Myspace to look for hints on Rose's page, but it's gone. "What happened to her MySpace?" Trish is the one I ask. "Her mom found it and saw what was on there and freaked out and made her delete it." I no longer have any ties to Rose. I have no choice than to let her go.

My appearance begins to soften over the next few months. I transitioned from punk to prep. I start wearing less makeup and recolor my hair brown. My clothing is less torn and has more brand names. I exchanged my ripped-up Converse for a pair of Prada sneakers I found at a discount store. I started wearing turtlenecks instead of band T-shirts. I urged my mother for a Gucci belt in order to match my new buddies. She says no, so I go to my grandfather, who reluctantly gives me the money. I enjoy going to school because I get to hug my friends in the hallways and everyone wants to meet the cool girl from New York.

Letizia senses my increasing social standing and begins to warm up to me. Even at night, she allows me to copy her schoolwork. Her mother leaves us off at the station every morning, where we freeze our asses off watching the sun rise. Letizia asks for a cigarette after I light one. "You better not tell your mommy!" I make fun of her. She sighs and rolls her eyes. She tells me she has a crush on one of the boys on the train with us. With his six-inch electric-blue hairdo and pounds of metal in his ears, he's difficult to miss. She waits for him at his stop every morning and makes me switch seats in the hopes that he would sit in the obvious empty position next to her.

He finally does it one morning. As I sit across from them with a sneer on my face, I can feel Letizia's heart palpitating. She lacks the courage to say hello. I tell myself that I'll teach her how it's done.
"Hi, I'm Julia." As he looks up from his comic book, he appears frightened. "Hi."

His lifeless blue eyes return to his reading. Letizia appears amused. "What's your name?" I inquired about him. "Alessandro," he murmurs, almost irritably. "This is my friend Letizia." Her cheeks flush brightly. He nods and looks at her. She manages to return the awkward wave. "I'm staying with her since my family is back in New York." Alessandro brightens. "You're from New York?"

The rest of the voyage was spent talking about music. He loses it when I mention Leftöver Crack, a popular punk band from New York. They're his personal favorites. Letizia is staring at me. As he steps off the train, we both wave. "So what did you think?" I inquired about her. She dashes off the train, whipping her backpack over her shoulder. I'm panting as I try to keep up and smoke my cigarette at the same time. "Are you really mad at me for that?!" I chase after her. She ignores me and continues walking.

While Letizia is at home playing computer games on Saturday nights, I go to the discoteca with my buddies. I wore skin tight Miss Sixty pants and pointed black stilettos. I put on a lot of shimmering eye shadow and straighten my long brown hair. To avoid smudging my makeup, I ride on Tatiana's off-brand Vespa without a helmet. We are not carded when we arrive. Instead, we are given a stack of drink tickets and led inside. We walk into the club and make our way to the bar. Barbara asks for a "Cuba libre." It's just another way of saying rum and Coke, but I enjoy the sound of it, so I get the same thing. We dance to the music of Gigi D'Agostino. When I notice

Alessandro's electric-blue mohawk waving in the crowd, Italian techno thrills around the dance floor.

I leave my companions behind and walk straight for him. In his platform boots, he towers above everyone. I lean forward on a stool and tap him on the shoulder. Squinting under the bright lights, he turns to face me. "American girl!" He appears to be quite different from the train. I wrap my legs around his body as he lifts me off the stool. As we dance, I can smell the liquor on his breath. He pauses for a second, and we lock eyes before he goes right into my mouth, swallowing my tongue and licking me all over. We collapse onto the couches, crazedly making out, drowning in one other's sweaty saliva. Letizia comes to mind. She'd despise me for this. I tell myself to think clearly. She would never have had a chance against him. And she's a total babe. nBarbara's cackle is audible to me. "Wait, is that Julia?" Oh my goodness! "Who the fuck is this dude?!?"

I get up from the couch and reposition my boobs in my bra. I cast a glance across at him. His spikes have faded and his lips are bloated. Barbara grabs my wrist and pulls me away before I can acquire his phone number. I suppose I'll have to wait until I see him on the train.

A few days later, I awakened to the sound of my phone ringing on the nightstand. I extend my hand. It's my mother calling. "What's going on?" Half asleep, I say. "They no longer want you there." "What exactly did you do?" She appears enraged. "What? Nothing! Why?" I'm fully awake now. "They didn't say anything. Simply behave normally. Say nothing to them about it. Okay?"

"Okay, I won't.", "Just stay at Grandpa's until I get there in a few weeks." Okay?"

"Okay."

She then hangs up the phone. I lay still, my heart pumping and ideas racing through my mind. What in the world did I do? Did Letizia find out about Alessandro and me at the club? Why do I muck up everything? Why is it that no one wants me? I can't sleep any longer, so I get out of bed and begin packing.

The trip to the station was quieter than normal that morning. I look out the window to avoid making eye contact with either of them. I move to the other side of the platform at the station and smoke by myself. I make a point of sitting in a different car when the train arrives. I'm embarrassed, abandoned, ashamed, and guilty.

At school, news spreads that I've been fired, and rumors begin to circulate. It was the smoking, piercings, clothing, and attitude. Essentially, I'm a horrible influence. The teachers mock me and refer to me as an "orphan." They assume it's a joke because I laugh as well.

Chapter 4:
HOMECOMING FIEND

When I arrive at JFK, I grab my bag and dash outside to breathe in the familiar filthy New York air. It smells familiar. I've started a cigarette and am scanning the throng when I hear a familiar voice. "Julia!" Trish is running toward me, her pink Converse sneakers trampling on the concrete. Her hair has darkened to a dark chestnut brown. I'm relieved to see Ace behind her. She leaps on top of me, knocking us both down. Ace leans down, my name shining in big bold letters on his bicep, and snatches me off the ground. I straddle him as he carries me all the way to the car, where Dougie appears to be relieved to see me."Where are we going?" I inquire once inside. "I got us a dope spot on the Upper West Side."

As we drive past my parents' house, adrenaline floods through me. I can see them moving around inside because their windows are open. I'm so close to them, but they appear so far away. On Riverside Drive, we approach a huge doorman building. Dougie takes my bags, and Ace leads us to a twenty-fourth-floor apartment. Except for a printer, a stack of paper, a paper cutter, and a bed, the flat is empty. A preppy boy in a bathrobe with acne scars emerges from a door holding a large blunt. "His name is Patrick," Ace says quietly. "This and the apartment next door are owned by his family." He's a private school student who wants to be a gangster."

"I'm having a party here tonight," said Patrick, "but y'all can crash for as long as you need.", "What's the printer for?" I inquire naively. "We're making money!" Ace states. "This printer is the only one in the world that can do it," Patrick boasts. He inserts a fifty-dollar bill into the scanner and perfectly copies it. I take it out and hold it up to the light. "It's not right," I object. "The texture isn't right. It's far too dry. "I'm going to need an iron and some butter or oil."

Patrick nods, dashes to the next-door apartment, and returns with butter. Ace looks on in awe as I take over the operation. I soak the paper in butter, then iron it dry before running it through the printer.
"The money feels smoother and more realistic this way." I'm not sure how I know how to accomplish this. I simply do. It's oddly instinctual. As I cut stacks of money with the paper cutter, partygoers start pouring in, pressing around me. Ace comes and goes, keeping a tight eye on me. When the blond girl with spectacles from 8th Street enters the room, I'm going through stacks of fake cash. "Hello, my name is Liana. "I believe we met.", "Yeah, I remember."

Her crop top and platforms have been replaced by a pink Care Bear T-shirt and shoes. It stands in stark contrast to what I'm wearing, which is a Gucci belt and black stilettos. She takes a nug of cannabis from her Hello Kitty lunch box. "Do you have papers?" she asks. No, I shake my head. When she sees my money producing station, she exclaims, "Whoa, what are you doing here?", "Exactly what it looks like," I add, laughing. "Should we see if it works?", "Okay, let's try the deli.", "How do you know Ace?" I ask her on the walk. "He used to date my friend but I just know him from around." We walk into the deli and ask for rolling papers from the clerk. On the counter, he places a pack of Rizla papers. I dig through my bag for the crumpled fake fifty-dollar cash. He raises it to the light before lowering it. "This is a fake bill," he declares. Liana and I exchange a flirtatious glance. "Oh my god, someone just handed it to us. Okay, forget it!" We're laughing as we race down the street when I spy a hot dog seller. "I have an idea," I say. I place my order for a pretzel and hand him the folded fifty. He looks at it, puts it in his pocket, counts out $48 in change, and hands it to me.

Ace bursts in with a beer in his hand, saying, "Where the fuck did you go?! I looked everywhere for you!" Everyone is frozen and staring at us. I take him to a walk-in closet where we can converse privately. Before I can say anything, he has his hands around my neck and is repeatedly pounding me into the wall. The rod falls to the ground, and I'm sure everyone can hear us. "You don't fucking leave without telling me!" he says, his teeth knotted. He goes away, leaving me on the floor in the closet, and I nod and fall to my knees.

I'm left on the side of the road, jaw gaping, astonished by this news. He rushes back into the passenger seat, and they speed away. Tears stream from my eyes and numb my lips as I meander aimlessly beneath the FDR, wondering if this was all my fault.

Ace's voice calls my name from the silver Honda. For a single second, I imagine myself fleeing and boarding my return flight, pretending none of this ever happened. As they follow behind me, I hear his voice again. "Come on! Get in! I'm sorry! "We're going to Trisha's!" he cries through the open window. I pause for a second, then raise my hands and walk back to the car. We arrive at Trisha's little converted two-bedroom flat in Washington Heights, which she shares with her father. "He lets me do whatever I want because he feels guilty about missing the first half of my life," she explains with a calm emotional detachment that I like. Her father, fortunately, can sleep through everything.

As we walk up the small staircase, a neighbor's door creaks open, and a little boy, no older than four years old, looks me up and down and whistles, "Wadup, ma?" Once inside, I'm greeted by thunderous Italian techno music and a snaggletoothed Chihuahua racing in circles. "Shut the fuck up, Gucci!!!" Tricia snaps. As she leads me to a filthy tagged-up couch, I maneuver my luggage through an obstacle course of soiled wee-wee pads. "Don't worry, it pulls out. Ace has spent a lot of time sleeping here." I cast a glance at him, and he swiftly turns his eyes. "Oh! And I constructed a drawer for you!" She excitedly opens an empty drawer in her scribbled-over dresser.

"Trish, can I have a word with you?" Ace says before I can thank her. His tone makes it sound more like a demand than a request. He walks out of the room, leaving her trailing behind him like a lost child. I sat in silence for a minute, wondering what they may be talking about. I start unpacking my luggage and neatly store the stuff inside the drawer. I locate my return ticket and take it in my hands. The door swings open. I instinctively crumple the ticket in my palms. I'm relieved to see Trish. "What ya got there?" she says. I put my finger to my lips. "Shhhh." She turns up the volume on her computer speakers. "This is my return flight. I might utilize it." Her smile disappears. "No, Julia, you can't leave again!"

"I know, but you didn't tell me he was crazy, Trish!"

"Yes, I did warn you! Rose was practically expelled because of him." When I hear the floor trembling from approaching footsteps, I hushe her. I stuffed the ticket under a pile of pants and closed the drawer. Ace bangs on Trisha's bedroom door. "Do you guys want anything from the store?" Ace spends hours in the store every time he goes. I shook my head. "Can you leave us some blows?" Trish enquiries. Ace throws a bottle across the room, which she catches in midair. She puts a chilly little pile of coke onto her desk and crushes it with her lip gloss and a MetroCard. "Shit. "Do you have a dollar?" I shook my head. "Let me get a tampon," she says. I read the graffiti that covered the entire couch as she left the room. I saw certain tags that I recognize. I notice one of her cushions is cleaner than the others, as if it had recently been flipped over. When I flip the cushion over, I notice my name in big red letters with the adjectives "ugly" and "dirty" next to it. My cheeks sting like I've been slapped in the face. I swiftly flip it back over.

Trish stomps back in, clutching the pearly blue perfumed tampon applicator like a trophy. She sips her coke and exclaims, "Whoop!" She tilts her head back to get the drip and hands me the applicator. I blow two big lines into each nostril. The powder seeps into my nasal passages and trickles up my forehead, all the way to the back of my skull.

My mind races as I bang my head to techno sounds on loop. Do they actually think I'm ugly? And who are they? And has Ace seen it? Can I put my faith in Trish? What will happen if people find I'm missing? What are my parents going to do to me?

Trisha taps away on the computer, exploring random females' Myspace accounts that all have "Italian Stallion" or "Proud Guidette"

in their bios, occasionally remarking, "I want hair like this" and "Do you think she's hot?" She selects their photographs and moves them to a folder on her desktop. I pick at my cuticles, waiting for Trish to leave the room so I can erase the defamation.
She notices herself in the mirror. "What's the matter?" You resemble a ghost! "Do you want something to drink?" Her manicured fingers dangle a long Newport 100, her blue eyes bloodshot and attentive. I can't help but think she's becoming her mother. She turns in her computer chair to face me. Her hurried voice conveys her anxiety to me. "Are you, like, not having fun here?" I'd like to tell her what I observed on the couch. "I think I just need a drink."

I grab a big silver graffiti marker from her desk and sloppily paint over the cushion after she departs. When she returns, the room smells like paint fumes, and she pauses to sniff around before looking at her desk. Her gaze shifts from her workstation to the couch as she hands me a plastic Big Gulp cup. I wrap my warm hands around it, silently watching the freezer-burned ice cubes melt into the vodka and orange juice.

I leap into Ace's arms when he finally returns. I'm quite insecure and rely on him to validate me. I bring him into the bedroom, where he positions me on the bed's edge and undresses me like a doll. He runs his tongue down my throat and across my chest. He kisses my belly button till his head is in my lap. He opens my legs and slips his tongue out before separating me like a flower, till he is completely covered in my juices. I gasp. "I've never done that before!" I'm speechless as he licks his lips and smirks.

"I know these are your favorite, the Double Stuf," he says as he hands me a box of Oreos. "You remembered?", "I remember everything you say."

This seemingly modest gesture has moved me to tears. We fell asleep that night entangled on Trisha's small twin bed, swimming in a sea of cookie crumbs.

The next morning, I find Trish on the couch and Ace at the foot of the bed, one hand clenched, the other grasping my return ticket. "I can explain that," I responded, my voice breaking. "You were planning on leaving?!"

I retreated into the comforter. "No, it was simply cheaper if I purchased a return flight." It was an excellent value!"
Trish keeps her gaze low as Ace rips my ticket into fragments and tosses them all over the bed before storming out. "I swear, I don't know how he found it!" Trisha's muffled voice says as I bury my head in the pillow.

I poke my head out from behind the pillow. Fighting back tears, I managed to say, "It's okay." But it's not acceptable. Nothing is fine, and there is no way out.

We'll be staying at Trisha's for the next three weeks. I'm late for my flight back to Italy. Ace fails to appear in court. "It's a trap," he declares. "They're going to take me back to Rikers Island." That private school pussy is facing serious charges. They're on the lookout for me."

Trisha's house quickly becomes a magnet for unsavory folks. Men dressed in basketball shorts. Men dressed in fitted suits. Some people have firearms. Some people use gel on their hair and tweeze their brows. Some have heavy New York accents, while others do not speak English at all. Ace occasionally leaves with them, disappearing for hours at a time. "Where does he go?" Trish is the one I ask. "I think he's just selling coke, babe." She switches the subject. "Do I need a boob job?" Take a look at this girl." She selects a huge photograph of a bronzed brunette. "This is the size I require. "A tiny C-cup."

She pauses for a moment before clicking on a new tab on the screen. "You can't tell Ace I'm helping you do this." Her long acrylic nails click away at the keyboard, quickly moving across it. "I can show you how to use the codes to make it like mine if you want." She gets up and lets me sit at the computer. I go through her list of pals and request everyone whose names I recognize. A note from an old middle school friend named Heather appears in my inbox.

"Julia!! I noticed a missing people poster with your face on it on 59th Street! Are you alright? Everyone is on the lookout for you!" My palms immediately begin to sweat tremendously. "Trish!" I scream angrily. She sprints over. Her eyes widen as she reads behind my back. "We're going to have to call Ace," she says. "No, I have to call Veronica." Trish wrinkles her brow. "Who's Veronica?" I pull my suitcase from under the bed and begin desperately searching for my Italian cell phone. "It's not here!" I exclaim. "What's missing? "Who exactly is Veronica?" I ignore her and continue sorting through all the nostalgic mementos from my life. "My cell phone is gone!" I exclaim. Trish gets down on her knees and assists me in searching for it, tearing apart the entire room. "Don't worry, Jules; you can always get another one." It wasn't even working here." I give her a chilly stare. "It has nothing to do with that!" It bears my best friend's phone number." I soften as Trisha's energy alters. "I think Ace stole it." I sigh in defeat. She gives a nod. "Me too." Trisha's phone begins to ring. Ace is the name. I take the phone from her grasp. "They are aware that I am missing. The cops are looking for me, and there are posters with my picture all throughout town.", "Do they know you're with me?", "I don't know but it's a matter of time.", "Don't be concerned, baby. I've got you covered. I adore you to pieces. "I won't let anything bad happen to you."

I want to yell that he has already done so, that I know he snatched my phone. But I put it out of my head and say, "I love you too.", "You are my Italian princess." What am I going to do? I'll go fetch all the posters and personally hand them over to you, okay?" I force a chuckle, but it doesn't make me feel any better. Ace arrives hours later, clutching a little stack of posters. "We drove up and down the whole city!" he boasts, brandishing the posters in my direction. "I look so ugly!" I say, yanking the posters from his grasp. Not only did they choose the ugliest images of me in existence, but upon closer inspection, I realize that all of my identifiable information is incorrect. My birth year is not 1992, I am not 5'9", and I surely weigh more than 110 pounds. Before Ace and Trish see how little my parents know about me, I crush the loose papers and bury them deep in the trash. It's humiliating. I immediately feel justified in fleeing. I made the correct decision. I'm now among individuals who care about me.

I nod, pretending to be interested as she scrolls through this stranger's Myspace page. "Trish, you're fifteen years old. You won't be able to get a boob job.", "I know but I have to start saving now if I want it!", "I want a Myspace page," I say, "a public one." I've been utilizing a hidden account to see what my buddies are up to., "Ace's not gonna like that," she warns. "Okay, but why can he be on Myspace all day and I can't?"

When Vinny arrives, Ace cleans up. He puts on a suit and gels his hair. I make fun of him about it. "We do business together," he dismissively remarks. Ace claims Vinny is rising through the ranks of an Italian crime family. "He's gonna be a made man soon," he boasts. "What's this I hear about a missing poster?" Vinny inquires as soon as he notices me. "How old are you, anyway?", "Sixteen.", "Is there a reward?" Uncomfortably, I shift. "No.", "Ace, let me have a word with you." I take my cue and quietly close the door behind me. I press my ear to the door and hear Vinny mumble something about "fifty thousand dollars." My eyes widen as a wave of paralyzing horror sweeps over me. I'm not going to let them sell me back to my parents. Ace would never do something like that, right? I have to put a stop to them. I push the door open. "If you guys think my parents would pay fifty thousand dollars for me, you're out of your fucking minds." I burst out laughing, attempting to persuade them to abandon this endeavor. "They don't even have that kind of money!", "Babe, we would split it with you!" Ace exclaims. "No," I answered, surprised. "It's not happening."

I slam the door shut, grab the phone, and race into the bathroom, closing it behind me. I hurriedly switched on the hair dryer to drown out the noise. My heart is pounding in my chest as I dial *67 and entered my father's phone number, my hands trembling with terror. As the phone rings, I secretly hope he won't answer so I can leave him a message, but the sound of his familiar voice brings me back to reality. "Hello?", "Hi, Daddy, it's me." My voice is trembling., "Julia? What the fuck are you doing? Are you aware that Interpol is hunting for you?", "Please! I'm ok! Please stop searching for me.", "Not until you tell me where you are!" I notice him becoming increasingly upset.

"I told you I didn't want to be in Italy any longer!" It took you three weeks to even notice I was absent! And you chose the most unflattering photographs of me for the banner! And all of the information on it is incorrect! You were never going to find me with that, believe me. Just stop looking for me; I'm OK. And if you receive a call regarding a ransom, don't pay them any money. I'm perfectly fine. Goodbye."

I hung up the phone before he could respond and turned off the hair dryer. I walk into the living room, pull a roach from the ashtray, and light it by the window, watching the world go by without me.

The bell wakes me up the next morning. I shuffle out of bed and into the living room, where I see Trisha's father, his huge belly protruding over his boxers, peering out the window through the blinds.
"What's going on?" I ask, yawning and hiding my mouth. "There's a fuckin' squad car outside, that's what's going on," he yells. "Get back in the fuckin' room!" I rush into Trisha's room and jolt Ace awake. "The cops are here!" He jumps to his feet and starts walking around, ducking under the windows and listening at the door. "What are they here for?" Trish inquires. "Could be me," I speculate. "Could be me," Ace speculates. When the buzzing stops, Trisha's father comes into the room and smacks her across the face so hard that it sends an echo around the room. As tears rise up in her eyes, she holds her face.

"Don't start crying right now!" We're the only white folks on the entire fucking block, and you and your pals are making it heated for everyone else! Trisha, that's how you get us all killed!" As he towering above us, I rushed to her rescue, placing my arms around her. "And you" He waves his shaky fat finger in my direction. "You and your boyfriend should find another place to stay." The party has ended. Pack your belongings."

"Dad, no!" Trisha screams. "You can't do this!", "It's okay, Trish," Ace assures her. "We have no choice except to leave. They are aware that we are present.", "Where are we gonna go?" I mutter softly, scared to arouse Ace's hidden rage. "I've got a spot," he says cryptically.

The location, it turns out, is Ace's childhood bedroom in his mother's small Bronx apartment. She greets us at the door, dressed in a pink silk robe and holding a glass of red wine and a lit cigarette in one hand. The setting is straight out of a noir film. "Ace! I wasn't expecting visitors! "The house is a shambles!" I take a look inside the pristine apartment. "This is my fiancée, Julia," Ace proudly displays his new trophy. "Wow! She's much more stunning in

person!" I lean in for an embrace, embracing her petite form and smelling the sweet cocoa butter scent.
"We're going to stay here for a while." "It got too hot in the city," Ace complains as he rushes by her, heading straight for his room, which resembles a frozen waste. Overflowing ashtrays and filthy boxers litter the floor, as if he fled in a hurry and never returned. "I'm not allowed to clean in there," she says quietly, raising her arms. "What can I do?"

Ace's mother is a shy, kind woman with jet-black hair and olive skin. She's tiny and modest, and in her spare time she enjoys reading romance novels and dancing to Puerto Rican music. She's nothing like Ace, and I can see she's on pins and needles around him. "He's just like his dad," she says to me when he snaps at her, and I feel bad for her.

He storms away into the night one evening, as the dust settles from yet another explosive battle with Ace, leaving me to clean up the debris. I gently collected the light pieces he tossed at me before dangling my upper body out an open window. My hair is tangled, and my body hurts. When I hear a gentle knock on the door, mascara-stained tears rush down my hot, puffy cheeks. "I'm going to order Indian food." "Do you have any special requests?" She opens the door, sneaking a glimpse into the war-torn bedroom. Her eyes widen as she notices the debris strewn over the floor. I nod quietly as she extends her small hand and guides me to the living room.

"You just get comfortable," she says, and "I'll set the table." I watch as she shuffles around the kitchen, only pausing to sip from her enormous wine glass. "What was Ace's dad like?" She comes to a halt and thinks for a bit. "He was very handsome," she says, her voice tinged with longing. "He had the most captivating blue eyes." It's where Ace gets his fair skin..." I nod as she continues. "All the girls were head over heels for him!" She raises her arms in disbelief.

"No one could believe he wanted to spend time with me. He was this big terrifying aggressive person, and I was this tiny shy little girl."
I have a feeling there's more to the story than what she chooses to recall. "Why didn't it work out?" I inquire, watching her smile fade to a scowl. I've realized that the answer is hidden behind years of anguish and remorse. "He had a bad temper." He'd shove me about. He broke everything in the house. When Ace and I arrived home one day, everything in the house was broken. The TV had fallen off the wall, the windows had been destroyed, plates, picture frames, and all of my clothes had been ripped up and damaged. He also broke everything in Ace's room." Her gaze is drawn to the ground. "It definitely frightened Ace. He could never relax again after that."

My thoughts return to my own upbringing, to memories of my parents and the enduring influence they had on me. A rush of pity washes over me as I recall Ace's rants. I recognize that he, too, is a victim of his upbringing. He can't stop himself from being violent. It's all we've got. "What was he like when he was little?" I inquire, determined to figure out what's wrong with him so I may fix him.

She's lost in thought as she transports herself to a different era. "He wasn't like the other kids," she says. "He was always serious and never seemed to enjoy playing with the other kids." His cousins would be having fun, while he would be glued to my side. He was odd. He just liked chatting to adults! And he was always so bright and artistically brilliant." As her thoughts wanders through the past, she grins, the good old days shining brightly on her face. "He was always drawn to nice things." The kid has great taste. Look at yourself!" She chuckles. I crack a grin. "I think he looked down on me because we weren't as well off as other people." But I always gave him whatever he wanted. I mean, everything I could."

When she notices an envelope on the table, her smile fades. Squinting to read the fine print, she goes for it and tears it open. Her face collapses in an instant. " 'There is a warrant for your arrest,' she mumbles, sighing as she sets the paper down. As she takes a deep swallow of her Malbec, there is silence. Then she turns to face me, a forced smile on her face. "I'll just leave this here so he sees it when he comes back," she says sarcastically. Shaking off the heaviness, she smiles and says, "I hope you like vanilla ice cream!" My gaze is drawn to the envelope as soon as she turns her back. My heart sinks like a stone. The letter is written to Simon Velez, a name I've never heard before. My veins are filled with rage and betrayal when I hear the name. I can't believe he made up his name! I can't help but wonder what else he's keeping hidden from me. I pluck at the tattoo on my wrist, his silly nickname indelibly engraved onto my skin, with trepidation.

Trish is no longer someone I see very often. Ace advises me not to trust her. "You saw what they wrote about you on the couch?" he asks, dismissing her frequent phone calls. He ignores my requests to go outside, visit people, or attend events. He spends his days on Myspace and World of Warcraft, oblivious to my existence. He's kept me tied up like a forgotten prisoner, never letting me leave the house alone. We only leave the house at night to get a slice of pizza, and we're always looking over our shoulders. I no longer recognize myself. I am a shadow of my previous self. My clothes are no longer fitting. My once-clear skin is now dotted with zits.

She's lost in thought as she transports herself to a different era. "He wasn't like the other kids," she says. "He was always serious and never seemed to enjoy playing with the other kids." His cousins would be having fun, while he would be glued to my side. He was odd. He just liked chatting to adults! And he was always so bright and artistically brilliant." As her thoughts wanders through the past, she grins, the good old days shining brightly on her face. "He was always drawn to nice things." The kid has great taste. Look at yourself!" She chuckles. I crack a grin. "I think he looked down on

me because we weren't as well off as other people." But I always gave him whatever he wanted. I mean, everything I could."
When she notices an envelope on the table, her smile fades. Squinting to read the fine print, she goes for it and tears it open. Her face collapses in an instant. " 'There is a warrant for your arrest,' she mumbles, sighing as she sets the paper down. As she takes a deep swallow of her Malbec, there is silence. Then she turns to face me, a forced smile on her face. "I'll just leave this here so he sees it when he comes back," she says sarcastically. Shaking off the heaviness, she smiles and says, "I hope you like vanilla ice cream!"

My gaze is drawn to the envelope as soon as she turns her back. My heart sinks like a stone. The letter is written to Simon Velez, a name I've never heard before. My veins are filled with rage and betrayal when I hear the name. I can't believe he made up his name! I can't help but wonder what else he's keeping hidden from me. I pluck at the tattoo on my wrist, his silly nickname indelibly engraved onto my skin, with trepidation.

Trish is no longer someone I see very often. Ace advises me not to trust her. "You saw what they wrote about you on the couch?" he asks, dismissing her frequent phone calls. He ignores my requests to go outside, visit people, or attend events.

He spends his days on Myspace and World of Warcraft, oblivious to my existence. He's kept me tied up like a forgotten prisoner, never letting me leave the house alone. We only leave the house at night to get a slice of pizza, and we're always looking over our shoulders. I no longer recognize myself. I am a shadow of my previous self. My clothes are no longer fitting. My once-clear skin is now dotted with zits.

When I express my displeasure, he dismisses it with a wicked grin, saying to me it's for my own good, that guys won't be drawn to me anymore, and he can have me all to himself. He lies to me about everything, and I lose track of what is true and what is a fiction of his imagination. What if I'm nothing more than a figment of his imagination?

I sometimes wake up in the middle of the night and he's not there. He disappears frequently, and when he reappears, he's always ready with a lengthy, perplexing explanation. Dougie's car broke down on the interstate, and he got lost on the way home after his phone died and he was locked out. I know he's lying, but I've learned to pick my battles well, and if I try to speak up for myself, I'm usually met with wrath. "We're fleeing! That should get through your thick skull. "Would you like to lock me up?"

Ace used to hug me after our disagreements, appealing with tears in his eyes. He'd drop down on his knees and beg pardon, swearing never to touch me again. We'd have passionate, explosive makeup sex after I'd forgiven him. I became addicted to it. Now he just pushes me aside and returns to his computer, his gaze fixed on the screen.

I'm not tied by intense love anymore, but I've threatened to leave him so many times that he scarcely recognizes my false warnings. I decide it's time to reclaim some of my authority. I begin to plan my escape. I gather the loose change thrown on the floor and recall the bus timetable to Manhattan. I take a look at the time. It's 6:04 p.m., and the last bus to the city leaves in eleven minutes. I take my bag out of the closet and start loading it with whatever I can find. "I'm leaving," I say as he taps on the keyboard.

He dismisses my statements as hollow threats, as expected, but I will not be intimidated. I zip my luggage shut, feeling the weight of the quarters in my pocket. When I see the time, 6:08, his gaze is still riveted on the screen. I dash to the front door and swiftly unlock it, quietly closing it so as not to scare him out of his Internet stupor. I dash along the corridor toward the elevators. By the time I click the button, I'm already out of breath. While I wait for it, adrenaline rushes through my veins. I return my gaze to the door, nearly expecting him to burst through it at any moment. After what seems like an eternity, I dash for the stairs, carrying my big suitcase down the flights.

My heart sinks as I hear the door creak open. I drop my suitcase and try to flee, but Ace leaps through the air, down a flight of stairs, and falls directly in front of me, blocking my path. He grabs my bag, snapping the metal handle off, and starts beating me with it. I cry in pain, pleading with him to stop, but he covers my lips with his palm and takes me up the stairs by my neck. I check the time once we're back inside the flat. It's 6:15.

A few weeks later, the doorbell rings. Ace hurries back inside the bedroom, tiptoeing to the peephole. "It's DTs," he says quietly. I leap out of bed and listen through the doorway. "We know you're in there somewhere." "All we want to do is talk," they yell through the door. "We can do this the easy way or the hard way!" They slip a card under the door, and when they leave, I immediately grab it. "We should just see what it's about, maybe they're looking for me," I said. Ace seemed hesitant. "We can't keep running, and it's not like they can arrest you through the phone," I'm saying. He hesitantly nods. I pick up the phone and call the number on the card, masking it with *67. "Put it on speaker," he directs. As we huddle over the phone, time seems to stand still. "Detective Malone speaking." Ace takes a breather, and I encourage him. "Hey, I believe you're looking for me. "You left a note under my mother's door."

"Ace, Ace, Ace, we've been lookin' for you, kid," Detective Malone confirms. "You've got a lady with you." Her father has been breaking our balls since she was sixteen. The DA will not seek charges if you send her home.'Because it appears to be kidnapping and statutory rape at the moment." Ace is angry with me. "I didn't kidnap her, she chose to be with me!" I consider the phrase "kidnapping," putting my head down to escape his sight. "Please keep the specifics to a minimum. Whatever the situation, she has to go home," Detective Malone states emphatically, throwing a ray of hope my way. "And you gotta come down to the station to sort a few things out."

"What things?" Ace inquires. "We'd like to question you about a fight that occurred outside a school a few months ago. Don't worry, we're not going to arrest you. We simply require your interpretation of events." Ace hangs up the phone and promptly calls his public defender. "Listen," his lawyer warns, "there's no getting around it if the cops want to talk to you." I'll accompany you in the morning."

Ace hangs up the phone with a groan. His anxiety is apparent, a far cry from the smug, arrogant tough guy I initially met. "I don't know if I should do it," he muffles. "We'll do it together. "I'll turn myself in first thing in the morning while you go to the station," I propose. We don't argue or fight later that night. Instead, we order chicken and waffles and spend the night laughing and making love while watching ridiculous Adam Sandler movies. I assist him in getting dressed in a suit and tie at daybreak. This is the first time I've seen him dressed like this. At first sight, he could almost pass for normal. "Don't worry, I'll see you later," I say into his ear as I put my arms around his slender form. Okay?"

"You promise?" he asks, his face as innocent as a child's.

On the long bus ride to Manhattan, I gnaw my nails. A part of me is anxious and fearful. The other portion feels lighter, as if a soul-crushing weight has been lifted. I stare out the window, my fear growing as we draw closer to Manhattan. When I get to the station, I take a big breath and say to the lady at the front desk, "Hi, my name is Julia Fox." I fled from my house. "I'm handing myself in." The lady snaps her gum and looks at me bewildered. "Umm, okay, wait right here." I sit on the linoleum chair and stare at the clock for what seems like an eternity until two officers come in front of me. One is bald, while the other is obese. "Well, well, there she is!" exclaims the bald one. "Come with us, please."

They take me to a small room with a desk and sit across from me. "We just want to ask you a few questions to make sure you're okay," the chubby one says. "I'm fine," I explained. Their gaze is drawn to the marks on my arms. "How did you get those?", "I bruise easily." I'm not being abused in any way.", "How could you do this to your parents?" wonders the bald one. "I didn't think they would care," I shrug. "What about your boyfriend, what's his name?", "Ace," the chubby one says. "Oh, right, that troublemaker.", "Can I go home now, please?" I kindly ask. "Your dad is on his way to come get you now.", "He is?", "Should be here any minute."

As they continue to grill me, I slouch in my chair and zone out. "What kinds of activities does Ace participate in?" Where were you two hiding? "Do you know if he has any brass knuckles?" My thoughts turn to Ace. He should be finished at the station by now. I only come when I hear my father's familiar voice coming from the main room. As an officer escorts my father inside the cramped room, I shift anxiously on my seat. When our gazes contact, he shudders. His expression tells me that he wishes he could slap the snot out of me. I'm glad there are cops nearby.

The stroll home is peaceful. He merely looks at me to shake his head and mumble, "You really pulled some shit this time, Julia." He walks quickly, and I struggle to keep up with him. When I go home, my mother emerges from her bedroom, scarcely acknowledging me or the injuries that cover my entire body. "You've gained so much weight," she remarks as I pass her in the corridor. I rush for the home phone and lock myself in the bathroom, feeling rejected. I call Ace's number, but it goes to voicemail. A sense of helplessness comes over me, and I feel powerless. "I'm going for a walk," I say to no one in particular before running to the Bronx bus stop.

By the time I arrive, it's dark outside. I press the buzzer, and I'm let in. I rap on the door. My heart is racing as I wait for him to emerge from the other side. But it's not him who opens the door. It's his mother, wearing her regular robe and holding a glass of wine.
"Julia! What exactly are you doing here? "How come you didn't call first?" I feel like a huge weight. "I'm sorry, but I don't know your phone number by heart, and Ace's phone was turned off." "I was terrified."

"Well, that's fine! "Please come inside!" She moves aside, enabling me to enter. "Is Ace here?" She turns her gaze to the ground. "They booked him, honey.", "What does this mean?", "He's awaiting the judge's decision." We'll have to see if they let him in the morning" I cut her off, my voice trembling. "Can I sleep here?" She pauses, and I feel like a stranger, like if I haven't been living here for three months. "Um, yeah, I don't see why not," she says ultimately. I force a smile, a sense of doom hanging over my head.

As I enter his room and examine the chaos, I instinctively begin cleaning, returning each object to its proper place. I push his worn boxers to my face, savoring the sweet-and-sour scent of his sweat. I can't help but feel like a piece of me is gone, like running your tongue over the place where a missing tooth used to be. I leaf through his sketchbooks, which are strewn with graffiti tags, doodles in bubble letters, and the odd masterpiece.

My eyes are drawn to his computer chair, which is now empty, and I settle into it, reveling in its old familiarity. I reach over and push the power button, but a password prompt prevents me from proceeding. I spot a clue option and select it, exposing the phrase "bloodz." I recall him telling me about his time in a street gang while he was in high school. I scratch my head, trying to recall what he said his gang name was. I recall seeing the words "Bloody Oz" scribbled in red graphic bubble letters on one of his notebooks. I type the words into the password box, and with a click, I get an entry to his secret hidden universe, which he has always kept away from me.

I examine his desktop, idly clicking on various icons, until my attention is pulled to a cluster of icons in the screen's upper right corner. I start reorganizing them, only to discover an untitled folder buried beneath. A surge of interest washes over me, and I clicked on it without hesitation. What I discovered astounds me: an entire collection of X-rated images. Some appear to be elderly. Some appear to be recent. I notice Liana in one of them, naked in bed between Ace and another female, her thick characteristic spectacles peeking out from behind a duvet as her friend's bare leg is thrown over his torso.

The mouse pad becomes wet with sweat as I scroll through the countless photos. My heart thumps so loudly in my chest that it drowns out all other sounds. Despite the pain each photo causes, I can't seem to stop myself from clicking. My gaze is drawn to a petite female with long chestnut hair, a spray tan, and the greatest boobs I've ever seen. She appears in a number of photographs, frequently with Trish. My thoughts race across my mind. How could they do such a thing to me? Was Trish involved? Did she stand in for him?
The worst part is that I can't even phone him to inform him that he is cheating on me. I had to push these sentiments aside and wait for him to leave, silently hoping for an answer.

Ace's mother creeps into the room in the morning and softly nudges me out of my slumber. She had no idea that I stayed up all night going through every document, album, and folder on his computer. I only slept for thirty minutes.

As she leads me out of his room, I cast one last longing gaze at the place I once called home, knowing I'll never return. The evidence I discovered has ruined the few nice memories I have of this area, and no matter how much I wish I could, I'll never be able to unsee it. I follow Ace's mother out of the apartment with a heavy heart, opting to leave all the embarrassing truths held behind those walls bchind.

On the bus trip to city hall, I'm straining to keep my rage under control when I blurt out, "Did you know Ace's girlfriend before me?" She looks at me suspiciously and responds with a nod. "Yes, why?" Before proceeding, I take a deep breath. "What did she look like?" She takes a breather. "Not nearly as pretty as you, don't worry." I can't help but smile when I hear her words. "Did she have huge tits?" Ace's mother nods, a sympathetic expression on her face. "Yeah, the poor thing had very bad back pain."

"I think he's still hooking up with her," I confess, barely above a whisper. She lets out a sigh and shakes her head. "Whatever it is, now is not the time to deal with it," she says emphatically. I nod and move my attention out the window, feeling a spectrum of feelings that are too complex to put into words. We spent the entire day at the courts, with Ace's lawyer, the public defender, advising us to remain there. "It looks better if there's people in the chamber," he says. As the hours pass, I feel myself progressing through the five stages of grief. When Ace is eventually called before the judge, I'm in the "denial" stage. At the sound of his name, I leap to my feet, studying him carefully as he shuffles across the room in chains, still wearing the crumpled shirt and tie from the day before. My rage fades as I notice how pale and unhappy he appears. He turns to face me just long enough to say, "I love you."

The judge does not appear to be as pleased to see him as I am. "How many last chances can a person get?" she enquiries. "We were extremely generous to you. We posted bail for you, offered you the program, and even allowed you to keep your freedom. You only needed to stop fighting. Have you ever heard the phrase "Fool me once, shame on you?" 'Fool me twice, shame on me,' you say? There will be no more chances. I'm returning you to Rikers. "There is no bail." She finally strikes her gavel. Ace whirl around, his shackles clanging as he reaches for his heart. "I love you so much," I say as I sprint toward the wooden railing that separates us. "Find a way to contact me!"

"Ma'am, you can't do that," yells a security guard. I'm afraid I'll have to ask you to go." I ignore him and concentrate my gaze on Ace. "Make sure my mom puts money in my commissary!" he yells as he is dragged away by another security guard. He walks into the rear room. His mother follows me out into the corridor. "That was like a scene out of a movie," she sighs. "I need a drink.", "We need to put money in his account," I insist. "Doll, it's going to take some time for them to process him." I'll continue to monitor the system. This path has been traveled before. You should go home and rest."

The air between us is thick with tension as we travel the 6 train. When we get to 86th Street, I give her a short hug before exiting. I walk past Kyle's place, where Ace and I first met, on my way home. I sit on the steps, mentally transferring myself back to the first night, when we took ecstasy and got tattoos, feeling unstoppable. It's not difficult to imagine that we'd be here just nine months later. We were doomed from the beginning.

I spent the following few days confined to the bunk bed that I now have to share with my brother. I lie there, gripping the house phone in one hand and the hair dryer in the other, trying to drown out the noise in the apartment, but especially the noise in my thoughts.

Whenever the phone rings, I close my eyes and hope it's Ace on the other end. My father grows concerned when he notices my disengagement. He storms into my room, a troubled expression on his face. "What became of all your friends?" You used to have a lot of pals.", "Shut up!" In excruciating anguish, I scream at him. "Get the fuck out!"

Four days later, I received a phone call from an unknown number. When I answer it, I am greeted by an automated recording. "A Rikers Island inmate... To accept the call, press the pound." When I click the pound button, I hear his familiar breathing on the other end. "Baby, you there?", "Yeah, I'm here," I manage to say before breaking down in tears. "Don't cry, baby. Don't worry, I'll get out." I regain control of myself and pay great attention as he advises me on his visiting days, what I need to bring for him, and how to deposit money into his account. I take out a pen and scribble down his inmate and case numbers, along with "Boxers no logo." White socks. White tank tops. Gray XL sweatpants. Gray sweatshirt. No red. "There is no blue."

The call is disconnected after a few minutes, but I know what I need to do. That night, I waited until my father was completely asleep before slithering into his room on my stomach and removing five twenty-dollar dollars from his wallet. The following day, I took two trains and a bus to Rikers Island. I'm assaulted with a terrible stink of sewage and mold as soon as we cross the lengthy bridge onto the island. The institution appears bleak and out of place against the bright background of New York City. They heard us around like livestock, yelling orders and frequently singling out someone for some good old-fashioned public humiliation. That person is sometimes me. I get yelled at because I don't have quarters for my locker, because my arms are bare, and because I'm standing in the wrong spot to wait for the bus.

But that isn't the worst of it. The worst part is the waiting. Fortunately, people-watching is excellent here. I finally make it to the visiting area after a few hours of being shuttled about, when I'm told to wait in an adjacent room surrounded by bars. Why do I feel like I'm a prisoner? I sit alone for an hour, watching people come and go before I'm called. I feel a tsunami of eyeballs roll onto me as I'm brought onto the floor. I'm shown to a little plastic table and instructed to wait some more. I see the bright murals adorning the walls, which I assume are there to make the youngsters feel more at ease. I sit in the small chair, and Ace emerges a few minutes later in a gray jumpsuit and plastic slippers.

I get to my feet and leap into his hug. I take a deep breath in. He has a distinct odor. A guard snaps at us, "No touching!" Ace immediately releases me, and we both sit down. His brows appear to be freshly tweezed and penciled in. My jealousy kicks in, and my mind wanders to a dark place where voices tell me that another girl visited him before and handed off provisions. He notices a shift in my energy right away. "What's wrong?", "Nothing," I responded passively. "You've only been a bitch for two seconds. Please refrain from doing so right now. You have no concept of what I require". I interrupted him. "Did you cheat on me?"

His pupils dilate. "Cheat on you?!," he stutters. Are you insane? When would I have had the opportunity?", "Please! You were gone all the damned time!" People begin to turn around as they see the disturbance. "To earn money!" So you could consume marijuana and eat Happy Meals all day?" He's now yelling. "I didn't wanna do that!!!" I respond by yelling back. "You made me do that!" A guard approaches us and reminds us that if we continue to argue, our visit will be terminated. I didn't travel for two hours and then waited four hours to get kicked out. I take a long breath and regroup before shifting the subject. "What have you been doing?", "Aside from fantasizing about you? Nothing.", "Did you make friends?", "There are no friends in prison, sweetie. I ran across a couple local guys, but I'm just keeping to myself and staying out of danger.", "That's good," I quip.

"There isn't anyone else, Julia." I just want to be with you. "I knew I was going to marry that girl the moment I laid eyes on you." I laugh and roll my eyes. "I'm not kidding! My soulmate is you. You're my equal. "I'd like to marry you." He snatches the corner of the visit slip and folds it up to form a ring. "Julia, will you marry me?" He takes my hand in his and places it on my finger. "No touching!" shouts the soldier as he moves quickly toward us. "That's it, buddy, visit's over."

Ace leaps to his feet and confronts the guard. Everyone turns to look at us. "If you don't cool it, I'm gonna put her down as banned!" The guard grabs his arm and turns his attention to me. "You stay here!"

Ace and I keep looking at one other as he's hauled away. I sit at the table, staring at the empty seat in front of me, trying to avoid the curious stares. I smile as I spin the paper ring around my finger.

Before leaving Rikers, I drop forty bucks in Ace's commissary so he can phone me. I begged my father to buy me a cell phone. "If you go to school," he offers me a deal. He enrolls me at Saint Vincent's, an all-girls' Catholic school in Midtown, on the advice of my grandmother, and buys me a silver Razr. I spend my days hooked to my phone, terrified of missing any of Ace's calls because of how he might respond. His jealous outbursts are becoming increasingly common. When I bring up the photographs on his computer and call him out on his falsehoods, he accuses me of being heartless. "How can you do this to me while I'm locked up?!" After a few weeks, I decided to drop out since I spent much of the school day trapped in a bathroom stall talking to Ace. I can't manage his emotional burden while also attending class.

In a matter of seconds, he goes from wrath to full despair and helplessness. I can't keep up with his constantly shifting moods, and I never know which version of him I'm speaking to until it's too late. I'm stuck on a roller coaster that I can't seem to get off of. He phones me constantly after I hang up. When I turn off my phone, he begins phoning my house phone and speaking with my father. I notice they've been having lengthy discussions. Ace even managed to persuade my father that he is genuinely trying to assist me. He's permeated every part of my life, and the only time I feel safe is when he's locked up in his cage at night.

He is always aware of what I am doing, who I am speaking with, and where I am going. He can sometimes tell me what color shirt I'm wearing. He warns me that he has me under surveillance. I'm losing my mind because I don't know who to trust anymore. Trish, who still had my Myspace password, was giving Ace images of my talks. This sends me into a tailspin, and I contact my cell phone carrier to permanently block Ace's number from calling me. Then the letters begin to arrive, each one more violent and horrible than the last. One letter in particular discusses in detail how he intends to murder myself and my entire family. He would first bind my father and younger brother to a chair and rape my mother in front of them. Then he'd dismember her body before killing the rest of my family before me. He planned to commit suicide as the big finale. The letters are generally accompanied by elaborate, lifelike drawings of devils and angels, as well as my naked corpse nailed to a cross.

I decide enough is enough. I'm going to say my goodbyes to him. I eventually picked up after weeks of him phoning the house phone. To avoid agitating him, I speak in a low octave, calmly and coolly. "I really believe I just need to concentrate on myself." Don't leap to assumptions because I'm not looking to date anyone else. This is not good for any of us. Please, you must release me.", "Let you go?" he asks, laughing. "I'm never going to let you go!" You are my property! I got your fucking name tattooed on my arm! Everyone knows you belong to me!"

"If you don't let me go, I'm gonna kill myself!" I begged him, tears flowing down my cheeks, frantic. "You're making me want to die, Ace!" You completely ruined my life!" I set the phone down on the counter. I can still hear him ranting incoherently. I feverishly pace around the room, opening drawers, until I come across a gleaming small box cutter. I take it in my hands and gash my wrist with it without thinking. "I just slit my wrists and I'm going to die, and it's all your fault," I say as I pick up the phone. I hang up the phone and fall asleep on the floor while drips of blood ooze onto the white kitchen tiles around me. When I hear the buzzer, I am startled. I stumble up to respond. "It's the police." I dash to clean up the blood on the floor. I put the razor blade in my back pocket and covered the gash with a long-sleeved shirt. I invited four officers, three men and one woman, to enter. "Is there a problem?" I inquire casually. "We got a call about a suicide attempt." "Are you the only person present?" I nod. "Where are your parents?", "Work." The truth is that my mother returned to Italy with my younger brother. My grandfather's health had deteriorated, and she needed to be near him. My father is staying with her for a few weeks to help her with the baby, but I can't tell them that. I believe it is prohibited to leave a youngster unsupervised. "Do you mind if we have a look around?" As they scan the apartment, I nod. "Can you show us your wrists?" They all crowd around me, and I hesitate. I raise my sleeves to see the bloody gash. "She's injured," one of the officers says over the radio. We require an ambulance."

I instantly withdraw. "No! Please! You don't get it, I'm perfectly alright! I was just annoyed! "I don't really want to die.", "We can't make that call," says the female cop. "Most likely they'll just sew you up and let you go home." I take a big breath and accept the circumstance. I don't have any more energy to fight with. At New York-Presbyterian, I'm transported to the mental emergency room for a comprehensive psych evaluation. The room is more of a stall, measuring little more than five feet by five feet and equipped with a rough plastic bed. There was no pillow and no bedding. This is a holding cell designed to be occupied for no more than 24 hours. I'm forced to stay in the cubicle for 72 hours because my parents aren't coming to pick me up. There is no phone. No TV. But, weirdly, I feel liberated. I'm no longer in a fight-or-flight situation. Finally, I can exhale. I have a sense of calm and quiet.

I like to write poems and draw images in my spare time. I read books and write music for myself. The nurses inquire as to when my parents will arrive to pick me up. "I think soon," I say, knowing full well that no one is coming. I'm secretly pleased they're out of this mess. Ace will not harm them.

They eventually escorted me upstairs to the eleventh floor psych ward. Every hue of green is different. Lime green, pale green, and hunter green are all shades of green. The fluorescent lighting makes the entire environment appear sterile and dismal. The windows are closed, and the strong odor of stale urine remains in the air. The room has one television in the center. It's turned off, but everyone is clustered around it as if it's going to turn on at any moment.

They take my clothes and jewelry, hand me mint-green scrubs, and walk me down a tiny corridor to the room I'll be sharing with Tiffany.
Tiffany declares herself to be a witch. She tells me she can tell I'm a witch from my aura after only a few minutes of meeting me. Of course, I prefer to trust her. She then asks me directly whether I want to be her girlfriend. Tiffany isn't particularly gorgeous, but she has a captivating stare. Her pupils are like long black tubes with no end, and her eyes are a deep dark brown, almost black.

In the psych ward, time appears to stand still. A ten-minute period feels like an hour, and an hour feels like a day. The main room has little entertainment alternatives, with little to do other than wander around in circles or play ping-pong. All of the board games are missing parts, and the seats and couches have dried pee caked on them that no one bothers to clean. The TV is only available on weekends, and the staff choose which movies we can watch.

Tiffany and I spend the most of our days smoking and hiding in the toilet. A guest was snuck in for her, puffing smoke into a ceiling vent. In an attempt to cast spells, we close our eyes, press our palms together, and channel all of our energy into one other. "Can you feel it?" she inquires. I'm not sure what I should be thinking, but I nod anyway. She casts a spell on the new girlfriend of her ex-boyfriend. My spell was cast on Ace.

I'm confident my spell must have worked after a week in the psych ward with no news from Ace. Then, one day, the guy who calls customer service numbers for every product he can get his hands on cries out to the floor, "Is there a Julia here?" As I approach him, I am overcome with fear. He extends the receiver, and I press it to my ear, listening intently before speaking. The breathing is familiar to me. Ace is the name. He tracked me down.

"How did you get this number?"

"I had to contact every hospital in town!" I was very concerned about you. "I thought you were dead." I keep silent, finding some solace in his familiar voice. "Are you there?"

"Yeah," I say flatly. "Look, I know you hate me but I really want to be a better man for you." His voice shakes. I can feel his agony over the phone. "You have no idea how unhappy I am here." I jumped the other day. They had to transport me to the hospital, and all I could think of was not dying before telling you how much I love you."

I take a long, deep breath. As I twist the cord firmly around my other hand, sweat drips down the receiver from my palm. I begin to feel

sorry for him. "Please, Julia, say something to me!" I only have one minute left on the phone.", "Why did you get jumped?", "I was hogging the phone trying to find you," he said. I grin. "You earned it. It's your fate.", "I know. "Are we still here?", "No," I responded.
The call is disconnected, and I hand the phone back to the complaint-hotline man, who has been tapping his foot over my shoulder. I can't seem to hit the ball when I return to playing ping-pong with Tiffany. My grip is wobbly. My thoughts are elsewhere. The phone rings once again. "If it's for me, I'm not here!" Across the room, I yell. The man on the complaint hotline rolls his eyes and mumbles, "I'm not your secretary," loud enough for me to hear. I keep one eye on him and one on the game, trying to be unconcerned. I can't understand what he's saying, but his body language says everything. He slams the receiver down, and it immediately starts ringing again. As he repeatedly smashes the receiver down, I notice him becoming increasingly irritated. I rush over to him, take the phone from his grasp, and yell into it, "Stop doing this to me!!!" Allow me to go! It's all over! You're a liar and a cheat, and you hit me. Please, just leave me alone!" I slam the receiver down and rush into my room, where the phone is still ringing.

My father is eventually reached by the physicians. He has informed me that he will pick me up on Thursday morning. The notion of leaving fills me with a rush of exhilaration. After 10 days, I'm starting to feel claustrophobic. The food is unpalatable. My meals are exchanged for glasses of rice pudding. I'm sick of the stink that gets caught in my hair and clothes. It's always there, no matter how hard I scrub. The hospital no longer feels safe to me, and I suffer panic attacks whenever the phone rings. But the outer world also frightens me. How am I going to avoid Ace? Who will I spend my time with? I'm very convinced Trish is a rat and has been telling him about my whereabouts.

I decided to phone Danny, a friend with whom I used to explore the Ramble. Hers is the only phone number I still remember by heart. I pause before dialing her phone number. We haven't talked since middle school. I'm embarrassed and embarrassed about my situation. When she hears my voice, she exhales and drops the phone. "You scumbag! What have you been doing?! You had us all terrified. Oh my goodness! My mother noticed your missing poster! She contacted your father and they spoke for about an hour."

"I'm actually in the mental hospital right now," I laugh to lighten the mood. "What?!" Her voice drops to a whisper. "Do you hear voices?"Because that was happening to me, and I needed a vacation from-", "No! I'm alright, despite the long narrative. I believe I'll be leaving soon. We should get together. "I'm missing you.", "Try to leave by Friday!" The party is intended to be a lot of fun! We can travel together!", "Yay! I'm looking forward to something!" This is the kind of normalcy I yearn for with every fiber of my being. "Are you still dating Ace?", "No. That's it. He is, nevertheless, enamored with me. He refuses to leave me alone.", "I only really know him because I used to blow him off as a cop." I'm sorry he left; I miss his stuff.", "I have to leave, but I love you." "See you on Friday!"

"Love you, bitch!" I hung up the phone, and the rest of the day went well. I consider what I will wear to the celebration. I fantasize about all the people I'll meet and friends I'll make, none of them will know Ace or anything else about me.

I get up early on Thursday. I shower and gather all the mementos from my stay: a journal, a beaded necklace given to me by Tiffany, a protective crystal, a pack of matches, and a few loose Newports. I patiently wait in the main room, facing the tempered glass doors. Today feels especially slow. I try to divert my attention by doodling in my notepad, but my gaze is drawn back to the clock. "Julia, your dad is here!" I hear someone yell.

I turn in my chair to see my father already in a conference room with a doctor. "How did he sneak in without me seeing him?" I mutter to myself. I rush up to the window and pound on it to gain his attention. I wave and say, "Let me in," but he just looks away. The doctor knocks on the door and tells me I'll have to wait. I begin to have a horrible feeling. Whatever they're talking about doesn't sound promising. My father seemed enraged. "Can we go now?" I ask as soon as they allow me in. They both pause to stare at each other after the doctor orders me to sit down.

"Julia," said the doctor, "we think you could benefit from staying a little bit longer." I leap from my chair, and my eyes well up with tears. "What? Why?!" I yell, staring at my father. "Sweetie, you need to calm down," my father replied calmly, as if he's dealing with a savage animal. "No! I've been here for two weeks! Did you know we can't open the windows or go outside? "How can a group of sick people get better while sitting under fluorescent lights with no sunlight or fresh air?"

The doctor cuts me off. "All we want is for you to get better, Julia." My colleagues and I believe Seroquel can help you. It's highly successful in treating your personality type"

"No! I don't require drugs! I had to go home. I have to start school. Tomorrow I have plans with a pal." I've already given up at this point. I know I'm not going home. I cast a glance toward my father. "You traitor.", "Can't she just take the medication at home?" my father inquired of the doctor. "We would need to keep her for observation," the doctor says, holding the contract that my father had to sign in order for me to be medicated.

"I'm not a guinea pig!" At the top of my lungs, I shout. "I am a person!" "I'm not going to take your drugs!" Two nurses enter the room and accompany me out. They placed me in a little cushioned room with a plastic bed. One of the nurses holds out a small plastic cup containing a large capsule. I cross my arms and shake my head. "If you don't wanna take your meds orally, that's fine," he said. "We have other ways." His gaze shifts in the direction of the bed, where I discover shackles. I open my mouth grudgingly. He spoons the contents into my mouth and offers me a cup of water. "Let me see." I open my mouth and extend my tongue. He opens the door and lets me out once he's satisfied.

I notice Tiffany playing Scrabble and take a seat at the table. I begin to feel dizzy and groggy. I take up the letters and begin to arrange them on the board.
"Uhh. GLOOP? Tiffany looks perplexed. "That's not a word," she replies. I burst out laughing, tears streaming down my cheeks.

I woke up in my bed the next morning with no recall of how I got there. I'm surprised to realize that I've been awake for sixteen hours. I dash to the phone and dial my father's number. "Please, Daddy," I said, "you have to get me out of here." "The medicine is far too potent!"

"Just do what they say, and they'll let you out," he said. I slam the phone down and dial Danny's number. "I won't be able to make it to the party tonight," I tell her. She seemed distracted and hurried. "It's fine," she replied. "I don't think I'm gonna go out anyway.", "Oh, okay," I responded, sighing with relief. "I made such a scene when they said I couldn't leave 'cause I wanted to go so bad." She doesn't say anything. "Are you there?", "Yeah. On the other end of the telephone, I have a call. "May I call you again?", "Without a doubt. Please remember!!" She hangs up, and I have the strangest feeling that something is wrong.

A few minutes later, the phone rings, and I answer it, believing it's her. "What's this I hear about you going to a party?" Ace asks in hushed tones before bursting out laughing. "I'm in a mental hospital," I think to myself. "I don't know what party you're talking about."
"Remember, Julia, all your little friends work for ME." Your best friends would sell you for an eight ball of coke. It's just heartbreaking. "I feel sorry for you." My heartbeat quickens as wrath rises in my chest. I tighten my teeth and say, "I hope you drop the soap every day for the rest of your life." I slam the phone down and call Danny again, but she doesn't answer. I decide right there and then that I will no longer be terrified of him. I'm not going to let him have that kind of power over me. I'm not going to give him the authority to keep damaging my life. I'm not going to open his letters, answer his phone calls, or speak with any of my "friends" who keep an eye on me for him. As soon as I get out, I'm going to get my tattoo covered. I am no longer his possession.

Chapter 5:
AFTERSHOCK

When I finally leave the hospital, my father enrolls me in a public high school downtown and I change my phone number. My father intercepts Ace's letters and hides them from me. I gradually begin to feel liberated from Ace's grip. He no longer controls my every move. He somehow obtains my new phone number, and the calls begin. I'll be able to screen those arriving from the island. It gets problematic when he has other people three-way phone me. But it has no effect on me. His threats are meaningless. I smoke so much cannabis and take so many medications that I don't give a fuck. When he tells me he's going to kill himself, I chuckle. I encourage him to do it by mocking him and yelling, "You won't!!!!!!!!" before hanging up. I'm not feeling anything. It's as if that part of my brain has been turned off.

Going to school is difficult. I can't seem to sit still. I can't concentrate. I'm known as the "weird white girl with a fat ass." I only have two friends, and I spend most of my days in the library reading books about child abuse or surfing the Internet in the computer lab. "Cheap apartment Hawaii" is my most frequently searched phrase. Veronica lives in Italy with my mother in her apartment. She dropped out of school to help my mother with my three-year-old brother full-time. She is now officially a member of the family. She called me one day to tell me she'd be visiting my mother for the holidays. I'm overjoyed with the prospect of having her here. I reunited with some old middle school pals who never liked Ace, and I reconnected with Liana on Myspace. She attends a nearby school, and we meet up in Tompkins Square Park to smoke blunts. Her outlandish costumes amuse me. The neon, leather, glow sticks, rainbow hair, fishnets, and makeup. She's a refreshing difference from the wannabe Guidettes I've been forced to hang around with.

I don't tell Liana I know about her threesome with Ace. I never bring up his name. Even though I have nightmares and occasionally feel like I'm being watched, I prefer to pretend he doesn't exist. I turn off my cell phone's ringer so I don't get triggered by the horrible little jingle I've come to connect with his voice. It begins to itch, and one day, after a few swigs from a vanilla Svedka bottle, I face Liana. "I saw a photo on Ace's computer of you and a blond girl naked in bed with him." She is surprised by my statement but responds truthfully. "It was the worst threesome ever," she confesses. I can't stop smiling. "I swear, I had no idea about you," she swiftly adds. That was all I needed to know. "Now that we're on the subject, Ace's been calling me, but I swear I don't answer."

"Why didn't you tell me?" I inquire, my suspicions aroused by previous betrayals by putative pals. Liana sighs. "He kills the vibe, bro." That's understandable. I began going out more frequently and purposefully befriending folks Ace had constantly warned me about, a graffiti crew he had labeled his sworn foes. It's my silent retaliation.

I've discovered that, aside from sleeping with these guys, I have a lot of fun with them. We hang out in dimly lit bedrooms that smell like bongwater and spray paint. The floor is littered with stolen bike parts. The walls are splattered with paint and adorned with crooked canvases. I find solace in the grittier chaos. We drink Sidewalk Slammers, which are half a forty and half a Four Loko, while listening to MF Doom, Wu-Tang Clan, KRS-One, UGK, Three 6 Mafia, and Mobb Deep. They all sell marijuana, therefore the blunts are the heaviest. We climb scaffoldings, scale structures, and hold wild parties in abandoned tunnels below at night. I get a buzz out of spray-painting my name all over town, and the boys like having me there to keep an eye on them.

It's eye-opening to be introduced to a whole new world downtown. These guys are all LES residents who know their way around the dark. They take me to CrowBar, Hanger Bar, Mars Bar, Mama's Bar, Kate's Joint, Max Fish, Lit Lounge, Pyramid Club, Iggy's, Boss Tweed's, and Blarney Cove, among other places. They like how creative I am and how I am always seeking for a come-up, and I like how they are always around.

Everyone with whom I hang out has a nickname, gang name, or tag name. I realize I have no idea what anyone's genuine name is. But they're all aware of mine. "JULIA FOX!" people yell as they ride their bikes by me or see me stroll into a busy room. When I stand semi-naked for a popular street artist, my name and likeness soon spread around the city. My painted body will soon be splattered across paintings all over West Broadway. I can't legally drink anymore, but my image is now on display in nightclubs around Manhattan. It even makes an appearance at the Gansevoort Hotel in a popular reality-TV spinoff show.

On weekends, I hang out with my middle school classmates from Yorkville. We went to high school parties in various apartments strewn over Manhattan, but the authorities always shut them down before midnight. We attend the infamous parties at Brooklyn's bedbug-infested McKibbin Lofts. We go to Lower East Side rooftop parties, punk performances, and raves, and we sip forties and Four Lokos in communal gardens and smoke joints by the river late at night.

During the week, I hang out with Liana and a large group of misfits who don't want to get up early for school. During the day, we go to free cribs and drink stolen wine till the sun goes down. We grab our complimentary supper at the Pink Pony and then go to Lucky Cheng's for cheap drinks. We bounce among Meatpacking District nightclubs, ending up in filthy after-hours venues all around the city with dodgy folks with money to spare. The celebration never seems to end, and it completely consumes me.

Liana and I make an excellent team. She usually discovers the party and pushes me to the front of the line, allowing me to work my charm and get us all in. Her credo is that with the appropriate group of people, you can make anything enjoyable, and we soon became collectors of rejects from all walks of life. After our wild evenings out, I wake up the next day with crumpled-up dollar notes in my pockets and bra, and my purse bulging with cash. Evidence of another good night.

My mother's name appears on my BlackBerry one night while I'm pregaming at a friend's place. She never contacts me. I turn off the music and pick up the phone. "He's dead." Her voice trembles. I want to pause not only the music, but also life, and rewind to five minutes ago, when I had the option of answering this phone call. Why is it now? Why has this happened now? The truth is that I already knew what she was going to say. I was aware of my grandfather's condition, but I was so preoccupied with Ace that I didn't want to think about it.

Except for a light unit spraying the ceiling in various colors, the room is pitch black. Red, blue, green, yellow, red, blue, green, yellow, red, blue, green, yellow. My buddies are all staring at me with their red Solo cups, waiting for me to say something. I hang up the phone, gulp from my cup, and re-start the music. I'm intoxicated, and the music is blasting, yet it's dead quiet inside. Just my thoughts bouncing off my heart's hollow walls.

I leave my friend's place and go to the gay club, trying to distract myself as much as possible. I take ecstasy and dance for hours, sweating to the music and grinding on strangers. I'm wondering if he can see me right now. What if, on his way to paradise, he had a sight of me in this homosexual bar with my tits out, snapping pictures with a coked-up drag queen, surrounded by porn magazines? He was a spiritual man with firm views and convictions. I'm not sure if he'll forgive me. But ultimately, I'm concerned about my ability to forgive myself.

My mother conducts a little service for only a few people. He didn't have many friends by the end of his life. My parents cannot afford to transfer me to Italy so quickly. Veronica takes my place during the funeral. I'm a little envious, but I know she's only trying to help. I'm overwhelmed with grief over his passing. I'm unraveling, and I just want to disconnect forever. I'd like to die.

Liana introduces me to Rick, Ace's ex-associate. They're now adversaries. Rick is a low-level PCP dealer and cocaine addict who still lives with his mother. He's ten years older than me, and his girlfriend attends the same school as Liana. She is five months pregnant and resides with her parents. Rick isn't particularly beautiful, but I enjoy getting high with him. And I like the indescribably exquisite feeling of vengeance I get whenever our lips touch. He lives around the block from my school, so I can easily pop in and out to get my fix. I smoke angel dust and play my favorite game, in which I pretend to be a dancer and tiptoe on the ledge of his balcony, hopping from one piece of furniture to another, never touching the floor.

Liana goes to a bar by herself on St. Patrick's Day and ends up meeting a group of Irish men from Ireland who buy her drinks all day. As the sun sets, they encourage her to board their limo and return to their hotel. I'm in Times Square with Rick and three buddies when she phones and asks that I bring drugs and females to the W Hotel. "They have money," she says into the phone. We're all in a taxi on our way there in a matter of minutes.

I get into the massive suite and discover cocaine on every surface. The toilet, the TV, the radiator, and even the kitchen counter. There are rolled-up fifty-dollar bills all over the place. I go around stealing them. Ash and Sara, the girls we came with, are amused. "Have you guys ever tried angel dust?" I scream at one of the men. "No, what's that?" he asks, removing a lump from his hand. "It's a brand-new designer drug." Here, everyone is doing it. "A friend of mine has some." I gesture to Rick, who has been floating about the room like a ghost in the shadows with a dust blunt in his palm.

The Irishman's face brightens. "I need to get some, I need to get some, I need to get some," he shouts maniacally, digging his hands into all of his pockets. "One bag is sixty dollars," I say. He takes out a wad of money and starts counting it. "Five should be good," I reply as he sorts through the large stack of twenty. "How much is that?" he inquires. "Three hundred," I answered, smiling and holding out my hand.

I smile and lean in to Rick after the transaction, muttering through my tight teeth, "That's six times what they actually cost, so you're giving me some for free." I extend my trembling hand, and he drops five bags into it. I take the Irish guy into the restroom and roll up a dust blunt for him. He takes a few dragons and is immediately transported to another dimension. He's so high up that he thinks he's in space. Because my tolerance is higher, I roll up another one. Then there was another. I'm getting worried because the Irish guy is running low on coke. I'm hearing techno music in my ears and I'm not sure where it's coming from. Rick is nowhere to be found when I exit the bathroom. I take out my phone and see it's entirely dead.

I dash from room to room, yelling his name urgently. "Did he say where he was going?" Sara inquires. "I think he went to get some more drugs," she speculates. I let go a little. The Irish guy follows me around, repeatedly declaring his love for me. As he wipes his wet nose with his palm, I'm starting to dislike him. His skin is translucent, and his entire vascular network is visible through his clothes. I can't understand him because of his grinding jaw and heavy Irish accent. When we run out of coke, Ash and Sara stand up and depart. "Are you sure you don't wanna come with us?" Sara inquires. An uncomfortable feeling creeps into the room as the sunlight peeks through the curtains. "I think I'm gonna stay with Liana," I say to myself. "I don't want to leave her." I walk them out, then go down on my hands and knees and scour the carpet for cocaine traces, wiping cigarette ashes on my gums inadvertently. I rummage among the ashtrays for any traces of a dust blunt. In my ears, I keep hearing techno music. I get to my feet and glance around. Who the fuck is listening to techno?

I hear Liana having sex with one of the Irish guys in the restroom. I'm starting to get antsy. I rush into the bathroom to hide because the Irish guy who is enamored with me won't stop talking to me, so I turn on the hair dryer to mute the sounds of Liana's nude body clapping against his .My stomach is cramping and my heart is pounding. Only Rock can make this right. I remove Liana's phone from her bag and notice that it's 6:30 a.m. I pretend I didn't notice and go through her contacts, only to discover she has no phone numbers saved. I remove my SIM card with my earring and insert it into her phone. I need to see Rick. I phone him repeatedly till he responds. "I went home," he explains. "Please stop phoning me. My mother is on her way right now"

"I just need to cop," I said, cutting him off. You are not required to return here. I'll make my way to you." I dash out of the suite with Liana's phone and onto the downtown train. The electronica in my ears is becoming increasingly loud. As people on the train stare at me in my barely there attire, a black American Apparel bodysuit and tight spandex leggings, their faces change into demons.

When I arrive at Rick's place, his entire family is awake. When I step into his bedroom, his mother rolls her eyes at me. I can hear her stomping and yelling in Spanish as she gets closer. "Ma, take a deep breath! We're not doing anything!" Rick hands me a dust blunt as she pounds on the door. I drop backward into the couch after one pull. The techno comes to a halt, and an ocean of black fills my view. I ask myself, "What is this?" Oh my goodness. What is going on? Then I hear a voice in my head say, "Julia, you're dying." I begged myself to hold on tight and not let go, even though I was warm and comfortable, not high, but finally at peace.

Suddenly, I'm whisked away on an escalating roller-coaster journey through happier times. My earliest memories begin at the bottom. The reel moves quickly, but I recognize the familiar sensation of being held by my grandfather. I noticed the tree that we planted in the garden. I see my brother riding his bike up the hill to our mountain cottage in Italy. As I near the peak of the roller coaster, I see myself, exactly where I am, in Rick's bedroom. It's as if I've floated up to the ceiling, and I can see a swarm of people swarming around me. Froot Loops are all over the place, and there's a puddle of milk around me. Rick's mother is praying over me in Spanish. I notice a pregnant woman digging through my purse and stealing Liana's phone. I made it to the top of the roller coaster. I clench my fists and brace myself for the fall, but then a window in the distance emerges in front of me. Light rays flow into the pitch-black space, illuminating a trail for me to follow.

My gaze is riveted on the window, which appears to be expanding. It has me spellbound, but whatever consciousness I have left warns me to turn away. When I let go of my attention, I notice light streaming in through the cracks in the hardwood floor. I can feel the heat on my face because it's so bright and close.

I woke up in the ambulance, covered in vomit. The paramedics are also coated in vomit. One of them hastily searches through my wallet, pulling out my phony IDs and holding them up to my face. "Which one are you?" he inquired. I shake my head and fall asleep again.

The beeping of my cardiac monitor wakes me up. My vision is hazy. It takes a split second to focus. When it does, I notice my father in the corner of the room. His eyes are bright crimson. He's been sobbing. I'd never seen him sobbing before. I feel as if I'm drowning in my own humiliation. Part of me wishes he didn't care about me so I wouldn't have to feel as guilty as I do right now. "I'm sorry, Daddy," I say softly. "I promise I'll do better." He is at a loss for words. "Man… you… you could've died." I tilt my head away from him, trying my utmost not to cry.

I felt reborn the next day. I feel as if I've been bathed with cosmic secrets. I'm feeling rejuvenated and revitalized. I called Liana on her home phone to inform her of what had occurred. "I glimpsed the other side, Lianna. God appeared to me. When we die, I know where we go. It's like a light-filled black hole. A swirl of energy." My speech is irregular and frantic. "I was so worried about you," she adds as she comes to a halt. When I got out of the restroom, you were gone, as was my phone."

"I know, I'm really sorry about it. "I'll hand you mine.", "No, it's not a problem. I robbed a girl and obtained a new one." I'm laughing. She never ceases to amaze me. "I'm glad you didn't perish." Maybe it's time to put the pipe away." I quit doing hard drugs for a few months and tell everyone I'm "sober," even though I still smoke a lot of pot. I am always on time for school. I finished my assignment. I take part in class. I even received the "most improved" award. It's the first prize I've ever received. I begin to consider the future. My buddies are all looking into colleges, so I am as well. I fantasize about fashion. I wander the streets of the East Village alone during lunchtime, visiting all of the vintage shops. Fantastic Fanny's for eyewear. Tokio 7 is a designer store. Metropolis is the place to go for fur jackets and leather boots.

Because my father brought a bedbug-infested chair into the house, when Veronica comes, we're forced to share a blow-up mattress on the floor. At first, I'm overjoyed to show off my gorgeous blond Italian closest buddy. I take her to Meatpacking District free cribs and nightclubs. It's a lot easier to go in with her beside me. Her accent is appealing to males, and she flirts with everyone who will give her their attention. She can talk about anything, and when she speaks to you, you feel as if you're the only person in the room. She is compassionate and attentive. While I'm in school, she creates collages for me. She proudly displays her affection for me by hanging the artwork on the wall. She writes me love letters in which she expresses her gratitude for taking her in and how meeting me has been the finest thing that has ever happened to her. I'm flattered at first, but it quickly becomes tiresome. She wants to accompany me everywhere, and she wears all of my clothes, causing them to deteriorate. I walked in on her hooking up with my good friend's boyfriend one night, placing me in the worst possible situation. "Why would you do that?!"

She chuckles and shakes it off. "It didn't mean anything." The sound of her voice irritates me. Things start bothering me that I never noticed before, like her wearing my pantyhose, her continuous cough from smoking so many cigarettes, and her perpetual runny nose. I've had enough when she starts acting like me, mimicking my mannerisms and attitude. I no longer feel comfortable sleeping on the same mattress as her, so I start spending more time at Liana's house, dressed in all of Liana's eccentric clothing. But no matter what I try, Veronica doesn't seem to catch the message.

During my absence, she and my father began to spend more time together. They visit the beach and take long walks in the park. He even takes her boating on his rudimentary sailboat. He buys her marijuana and takes her photo in front of the sunset, as if I don't exist. Her mother constantly phones our house, pleading with her to return to Italy. Veronica is stabbed in a random incident uptown one night. A masked man crossed the street diagonally, went up behind her, and slashed her neck with a knife. She seized the sword and threw him off, but not before he slashed through all of her fingers' tendons. She was transported to the hospital for emergency surgery. I set aside my emotions and show up for her. My father is already conducting the inquiry and seeking to uncover security footage when I arrive at the hospital.

When she comes home from the hospital after surgery, she is gracious enough to share her pain medicine with me. This postpones our impending expiration date and allows me to bear the circumstance for a little longer. When Veronica's mother learns of the attack, she rushes to New York. Liana joins me for a lunch meeting with Veronica's mother and Veronica, who arrives late with my father. She fidgets with her cast as her mother begs her to return home. When her mother begs me to advise her to go home, Veronica and I avoid making eye contact. "I don't want to make things awkward between us," I add softly. "I just need my space back."
"I'm now a guest of Tom's," she shrugs. He told me I could stay. Right?" She looks to my father for support. I give him a wary look, but he nods and says, "I'm not kicking anyone out." What can I do if she wants to stay?"

The dinner has yet to arrive when I rise up and say, "Come on, Liana, let's go." Liana is irritated that she would miss out on the free supper and reluctantly stands up. As we move away from the table, Veronica's mother begs me to stay in Italian. When I return to Liana's house, I lock myself in the bathroom and contact the immigration hotline to notify them that an illegal alien from Italy has established residency in the United States. After a half-hour of waiting, I come to the depressing understanding that rich blond girls are not on the deportation radar of US Immigration.

I quickly called my mother after returning to my father's place. My goal is to tell her that my father is financially supporting Veronica, knowing that this will irritate her. And I am completely correct. "If you don't want her there, she has to leave," my mother replied flatly. I rush into the bedroom, the house phone still in my hand, and stand over Veronica as she paints her toes with my nail polish.

"You have to go," I tell her, emotionless. Her equally deadpan expression irritates me. "Come on, pack your shit." My father appears through the doorway. "My mom says you have to go!"

"Fuck your mom," she exclaims. How could she say anything negative about my mother? I lunge at Veronica. I grab her hair and slap her in the head repeatedly, clawing her face and breaking three acrylic nails in the process. My father yanks me away from her, threatening to call the cops on me. I abandon her sobbing on the floor. I turn to him, trying hard not to cry, and say, "It's either me or her, or I'm leaving and I swear to God I'm never coming back."

"Calm down, sweetie, just calm down." I understand what this means. "I fucking hate you," I scream, my voice shaking with rage. He takes a breather and replies, "I love you too, sweetie." I pushed him against the wall, encircling him and yelling, "Give me money! I require funds! "I'm going!" As he pulls out his wallet and hands me four crisp hundred-dollar bills, I wave my bleeding palm in his face. He's given me the most money he's ever given me. This is the final goodbye.

As I quickly gather my possessions, I try to appear stoic. I'm curious if my mother stayed on the phone through it all. I'm curious if she heard me defending her. I hope she is proud of me. My baggage and clothes are stuffed into a few little "I ♥ NY" plastic bags. I grab Fernando, my cat, and flee out of the apartment barefoot. I make it to a pay phone and dial Liana's number, hoping she answers. She's my last hope. Fortunately, she detects the first ring. "Hey, I have to move in with you," that's what I say. "Who is this?" she wonders. "Julia!"

"When do you wanna move in?", "Now.", "Great, can you get a dutch on the way?", "Vanilla?", "Yeah.", "Okay, I'm biking now." In the sweltering July heat, I hop on my candy-colored hundred-pound cruiser and pedal from the Upper East Side to Greenwich Village, struggling to balance the plastic bags on my handlebars and Fernando in my basket. Fernando jumps out of the basket and onto my chest, sinking his sharp little claws into my flesh as we both hold on for dear life as we both drive down Park Avenue. I can't stop or we'll topple over. So we ride the rest of the way like that, as I scream my eyes out for many reasons.

Dina, Liana's mother, is an even worse hoarder than my father. There are mounds of useless trash all around the place that she claims is precious. We had to crawl over mountains of garbage and awkwardly arranged furniture to get to the kitchen and bathroom in the small railroad apartment off Bleecker Street. The "bedroom" is an area of the flat divided with white poster board. I share a bunk bed with Liana. Every wall has a shoe rack filled with mismatched shoes that haven't been used in years. Every surface is covered in clothes and fancy jewelry.

Dina sells jewelry on a folding table on Broadway during the day. I pay her visits and bring her coffee and pizza. It's entertaining to see her push people away from her booth while she introduces me to the other sellers on the block. "This is my daughter Juliana," she cries, her accent thick and uncertain.

I love the lovely feminine vibe that Liana and Dina exude. It's a far cry from the icy, toxic masculinity I'm used to. Liana and I begin telling everyone we're sisters, and it doesn't feel like we're lying-it's as if we've always been sisters. I feel as if I've known her since the dawn of time. Her hair is naturally curly, but she straightens and bleaches it platinum blond. Her lovely face is hidden behind heavy spectacles, and she carries a little extra weight on her frame, with stretch marks on her skin and her belly peeking out over her miniskirts. Nonetheless, she glances in the mirror and triumphantly declares, "I look fucking amazing," before donning a twenty-dollar fur coat from a thrift store. She exudes strength and self-assurance. It's my favorite aspect of her. I wish I was more like that.

Chapter 6:
MASTERMIND

The next day, I arrive at the quiet Chelsea building and press the basement buzzer. I pause before proceeding down the dirty, barren steps. I notice the stench, which is a unique combination of sewage, smoke, urine, candles, and Lysol. I'm greeted at the foot of the stairs by a 300-pound Ukrainian woman in her mid-forties seated at a little desk. As I approach the room, she doesn't acknowledge me, so I creep close to her, take a big breath, and extend my hand. "What do you want?" she asks, her voice heavy with an accent. "My name is Julia-I mean Valentina-Ronald said to come here?"

She looks at me, then nods curtly. "My name is Greta, I manage here." When the buzzer goes off, she swats me away with her hand like a mosquito. I take a seat on one of the couches in the lounge, attempting to blend in. When I try to strike up a conversation with a lovely redhead, she turns her back on me, leaving me hanging in mid-sentence. The girls move about the room as if I don't exist. Nobody ever asks me my name. Nobody even bothers to look at me. I got the impression that they don't like me, that this was a horrible idea. Greta walks in just as I'm starting to reconsider everything. "Valentina, you're up," she yells, snapping me out of my reverie. I stand up awkwardly and stare at her, not knowing what to do next and too afraid to ask. "What are you waiting for?!" she exclaims. "Get dressed!"

I dash to my suitcase and quickly dig through everything. What exactly am I looking for? I'm not certain. I emerge from the restroom a few minutes later, wearing a cheap, mismatched black cotton thong and bra, tattered pantyhose, and bright red lipstick. "She looks like a hooker," someone snickers as I leave the room. "He only likes new girls," Greta adds as she records data in a notebook. She becomes animated with hate as she finally looks up to see my attire. I can hear the girls laughing as she makes funny faces and waves her huge arms around. "Valentina. What exactly are you wearing? Valentina, this is a high-end establishment! You appear to be a cheap hooker!"

She motions for me to go change by pointing to a shadowy locked door behind her desk. My cheeks sting from shame as I walk past the wall adorned with paddles, whips, shackles, ropes, and chains. When I open the door, I find myself staring down an endless corridor of darkness. All I see in front of me are a few black heavy-duty garbage bags that smell strongly of latex, lubrication, and piss. I take a few careful steps down the dimly lighted corridor, sweat pouring down my brow as I struggle to hear Greta's shrill cry. "To the left!" she orders, and I rush to comply, my heart racing in my chest. I push open the next door with shaky hands, turn on the light, and my jaw drops. A phallic utopia awaits me in the form of a walk-in closet. Dildos of various sizes, shapes, and colors cover the walls from top to bottom. White and little. Pink and wavy. Black and massive, bigger than my arm. There are thick ones, thin ones, electrified ones, even two dicks in one. I quickly learn that the dildos are kept in the hallway in case the cops decide to raid the property... again. "No dildos, no penetration, no problem," Greta retorts casually.

My gaze is drawn to the clumsily hung costumes strewn behind a towering display of dicks as it scans the untidy area, and I cringe.

Greta's impatient energy permeates the room as I hurriedly rummage through the rack. Everything is either excessively large or stinks of body fluids. I located a low-cost plastic nurse's uniform, a nun costume from a Halloween store, and a wrinkled schoolgirl's skirt. None of this is effective. I eventually locate a gleaming latex catsuit, but when I slide it over my feet, I see a few stains at the ankles that resemble crusty jizz. I start to stress because I feel like I'm going to puke.

I eventually settled on a black corset and a black tube top that I repurpose as a miniskirt. I quickly put on a pair of old, worn-out peep-toe platform sandals a size too big and head out as Mistress Valentina. It's not the glamorous entrance I had envisioned, but it'll suffice for now. "Two hours, Xing Palace, his name is Stewart, and he likes smoking." Greta uses her pointed and stubby finger to gesture down the corridor. I nod, but I'm still not sure what I'm doing. "First door to the right."

I take her directions and proceed down the hall. The clacking of my big heels reverberates down the deserted corridor. I walk as slowly as I can in order to save even a few minutes off what I expect to be the longest two hours of my life. I halt in front of the Xing Palace door, my hand on the doorknob. I take a few deep breaths, fearful of becoming this stranger's good time.

A thick cloud of smoke engulfs me as soon as I open the door, wrapping itself around me and sucking me in. I squinted through the haze into the dark room, hoping to find him. I'm taken aback as I look down and see him unmoving on the floor beneath me.

With my heart pounding, I hurriedly exclaimed, "Oh my God, I didn't see you there."

"I sincerely hope you don't mind," he says. "I hooked myself up to save us some time." As I go closer, I notice he's fully naked, and his balls are tightly bound to a rope that's attached to a torture device suspended from the ceiling. "My name is Stewart. 'Smoking Stewart,' they call him. "However, my friends call me Stew."

"Nice to meet you," I said quietly say.

My first impression of him is of a man in his fifties, out of shape, with a pasty skin and a downward gaze. I also see he has a little penis. Two packets of cigarettes, Camel Lights and Marlboro Lights, lie on the floor near him. "Those are for you," he tells her. "I didn't know which you prefer, so I got you both." I don't tell him I'm a Newport smoker. I don't want to offend his sensibilities. I lit a Marlboro and smoked it to soothe my nerves. My hand trembles slightly as I hold the cigarette to my lips, but he cuts me off before I can take another drag. "You might want to save that for me," he replies, his voice muffled by the black rubber mask he's just slipped on. "You're going to have to do a lot of smoking."

In startled silence, I watch as he attaches a rubber tube to the mouthpiece of the mask and explains in a distorted voice that I am to chain-smoke the cigarettes and blow the smoke through the tube, which will be in his mouth. "And if you're up for it, you can spit in my mouth or even pee." I take another inhale and expel the smoke through the tube, a strange mix of discomfort and detachment washing over me. My curiosity gets the best of me as I kneel over him, dutifully blowing the cigarette smoke into the tube. I began to study him, paying close attention to every part of his anatomy. I've never been so close to an elderly man before, and it's both unpleasant and interesting.

I observe his hair plugs, the elevated pimples on his arms, and the stretch marks on his tummy. Axe body spray and sweat cling to his skin, mingling with the acrid odor of burning cigarettes. I try not to gag when I see his little, flaccid penis dangling limply between his big legs. I try to pass the time by making small chat and asking him questions about himself in between exhales. "Where are you from?" I inquire. "I'm a New Yorker!" he exclaims as he spits the slimy tube out of his lips. I grew up in a lovely region of New Jersey."

"But you live here now?" I will follow up. "No, I actually live in New Jersey with my mother." "She enjoys having me around," he shrugs. "You should come over to the house sometime." He thought he needed a rest after an hour. "Hey, do you like the Strokes?" he says as he pulls a small speaker from his duffel bag. "They were the first live concert I ever went to!" I responded, delighted that we might be able to listen to some decent music to brighten the mood. "This is me and my cover band!" he exclaims, a toothy grin on his face. My joy immediately fades as he starts to play his rendition of every single Strokes song. He sings along with the songs, occasionally shouting them out a cappella. He clearly believes he has a fantastic voice. Cringing from secondhand embarrassment, I force a smile and bop my head to the music. "Okay, let's get back to it!" he exclaims, clapping his fists.

He gets back on the floor, and I resume smoking and puffing smoke into the tube. As the minutes pass, I can feel the smoke searing the back of my throat and my fingers turning yellow. The dreadful music continues to play, the man screams, and the smoke and discomfort begin to affect me. My bloodshot eyes are throbbing with a pounding headache, and my back and knees hurt from crouching for so long. I steal looks at the digital clock on the corner, but time has stopped and the minutes seem to stretch on for hours.

I stopped smoking after the tenth cigarette. My tongue is on fire, and I am dizzy and faint. I can't help but wonder why he doesn't just light up a cigarette and why he hasn't gotten a boner yet. Is there something I'm missing? I become increasingly frustrated, and the desire to kick him in the dick begins to dominate me. I realize I need to pee and recall what he stated at the start of the session. I find a little funnel in his bag of tricks and insert it into the tube. I crouch down, towering above him, and release my bladder into the funnel. As the golden fluid drips down his face, he gargles and gags. "Mmmm," he moans, and I realize he's finally getting an erection. "Do you like porn?" he asks, spitting out the tube. "Yeah, of course, who doesn't like porn?!"

At this point, anything beats chain smoking on my knees. He stands up, drenched in urine, and walks over to his laptop. He has a long queue of stored videos on it, all of which are of older men forcing themselves on meek younger-looking males. He jerks away furiously, maniacally skipping from video to video, occasionally asking for my input. I sit uncomfortably next to him because he doesn't seem to need me, but since he's paying for my services, I decide to attempt something.

"I bet you wanna suck that big cock like a little slut, don't you?" I say this gingerly, unsure whether he's accepted his obvious queerness.
He furiously nods, his head jerking back and forth. "Uh-huh," he whimpers, before his body convulses and he splatters all over his hand. I get an odd sense of triumph and pride. I know exactly what he wants! I'm aware that part of my job entails reading between the lines. I need to know what they want before they've even decided on it. I've figured out the trade's secret.

When I look him in the eyes and promise him that if he comes to see me again the next night, I'll have a fresh load of jizz to feed him, he's overjoyed. The next day, I pay a girl $20 to make her client come into a condom and hand it over to me. I tuck it away in the back of the fridge while I wait for Stewart. That night, my plan comes to fruition, and he becomes my regular. He comes practically every night and departs if I'm working with another client. He is devoted to me. It's a brand-new sensation. He's growing on me. I'm starting to look forward to our meeting. He even offers to let me live in his New Jersey house and recommends we have a kid together.

"I just know my mom would love you," he says.

Chapter 7:
BILLION-DOLLAR BABY

I wake up one morning after six months in the dungeon and decide today is my last day. I'm going to give up. I've accumulated enough regulars that I can see at my place, and if all else fails, I can always be a stripper. At the very least, it would not necessitate the same mental gymnastics as BDSM.

I've arrived at the dungeon, striding boldly into the lounge, ready to say my goodbyes, when Greta cries out, "Valentina! You've received an outcall. Rich guy, classy guy." "Dress elegantly, Valentina," she says with a wink. "There is no hooker." I've never done an outcall before, but they're well-paid, so I nod and rush back to my locker. I uncover a Victoria's Secret maxi dress with a terrible floral motif while rummaging through my collection of Sixth Avenue sex-shop lingerie and throw it on. I pack a large bag of tricks, call a cab, and ride uptown.

When I arrive at The Union Club, I am stopped at the entry and told to enter through the service door. Looking down at my modest attire, I can't help but worry if they believe I'm a prostitute, despite the fact that I'm wearing a floor-length gown. I go upstairs and stroll along the long corridor, carefully inspecting the endless rows of photographs of old white guys. This location is the polar opposite of seductive. It has a spooky and haunted sense about it. The musty odor, peeling wallpaper, and soiled carpet indicate that the space is in desperate need of a makeover.

My sweating fingers hold the creaking brass doorknob as I stand outside the door. I take a long breath, attempting to evacuate some of my nervous energy. The dungeon is a monitored setting, and the management checks in on a regular basis. This place feels deserted, and I'm alone. I hear glasses clinking and someone moving around inside the room. I gather my confidence and knock on the door. It swings open to reveal a man in his late forties with tanned complexion, jet-black hair, enormous brown eyes, and a pleasant smile that stretches from ear to ear. He draws me in and kisses me twice on each cheek as I extend my wet hand. Rohan is his name, and he introduces himself. His accent is distinct, Indian with a touch of something else I'm not sure what it is, but it sounds rich.

I excuse myself and dash to the toilet to reapply my MAC Ruby Woo red lipstick, let my hair down, and slip into my little black dress and heels. When I come out, he's holding a platter of strawberries and whipped cream. He pours me a glass of champagne, and we raise our glasses to "new friends." His look follows me long after I've finished speaking, yet he's extremely endearing.

Rohan pulls a chair next to me as I take a seat on the couch. He begins to describe how he stumbled across my photograph and was reminded of his childhood lover, whom he claims was the love of his life. "You remind me of a younger Sophia Loren!" he cries, his joy apparent. He becomes much more enthusiastic when I tell him I'm Italian. "I could move to Italy with you tomorrow!" he declares triumphantly. His demeanor is dramatic, exaggerated, and passionate. He is a natural storyteller as well as a visionary.

After an hour of talking, I'm wondering when we're going to start this program. "So, what's your fetish?" I ask directly. "My ex-girlfriend, we just broke up not long ago," Rohan says after a little pause. She told me she had been a dominatrix before we met"

"So basically you're trying to find her again." I interrupted him, feeling encouraged by the cocktails. "Like a new version of her, her but not her.", "I must say, that is a wonderful analysis. "You are such a wise young lady." Rohan is clearly taken with me. I blush, recognizing that I frequently receive compliments on my appearance but never on my intelligence. "Do you mind if I smoke a cigarette?" I inquired about him. "Please, make yourself at home." Rohan stands up to grab me an ashtray, and I'm taken with him. I've never felt more at ease and safe with a man. Our discourse has no bounds. We cover everything. He wants my opinion on his children, two daughters who are younger than he is. He says they're acting out, and I tell him not to punish them because they're definitely dealing with something more serious. He respects my opinion as if I were his equal. I can tell because of how closely he listens to me and recalls everything I say. He's a refreshing contrast from the insecure American men I'm compelled to associate with.

I don't look at my phone for six hours while we converse and laugh nonstop. When I do, I notice fifty missed calls from the dungeon.
"I have to go," I reply, a sad expression on my face.
He appears to be disappointed as well. "May I drive you back downtown?"

"I thought you'd never ask." He plays loud opera music and occasionally yells out lyrics in terrible Italian during the ride. I laugh awkwardly, but the reality is that this crazy eccentric man amuses and intrigues me. When we get to the dungeon, he parks the car and we sit in silence, neither of us knowing what to say next. "You should take my number, 'cause I'm quitting this place," he says. I take his iPhone and save my name as Valentina/Julia.

I haven't heard from him in a few days. I'm not sure about it. It is not uncommon to develop a relationship with a client, but they will usually talk themselves out of going beyond the business transaction. After all, I'm only a prostitute. I still pray at night for a sugar daddy to save me from this life of servitude.

He finally calls, and we agree to meet for lunch the next day. I'm so nervous that I spend the entire night deciding what to wear. Nothing about me shouts "classy" or "sophisticated." All of my outfits resemble those of a high-class escort. I try on dozens of clothes before settling on a white knit tank top that falls low enough to reveal my ample cleavage, tight jeans, and a pair of thrifted Roberto Cavalli wooden platform wedges.

When I arrive at the restaurant, he is already seated at the table. He rises up as soon as he sees me and does not sit down again until I do. As his gaze moves across my body, collecting every detail, I blush. He lavishes me with so many compliments that I feel like the most beautiful, brilliant girl in the world when I'm with him. "I love the way you speak," he remarks. "It's very Italian." It's almost like a song." He's blown away by how well I speak Italian. "You must teach me!" he exclaims. When he finally asks how old I am, I lie and tell him I'm twenty, despite the fact that I'm only nineteen. I made the decision not to tell him I'm still in high school. That would raise a red signal for a man of this type, in my opinion.

As I eat my lunch, I can't help but notice the hostess's judgmental stares and ugly looks that I just seem to be getting. "So, what's your plan now that you're no longer working at the dungeon?" asked the man. "I'm not sure. To be perfectly honest, I just want to get a lousy automobile and go around the country seeing everything." He laughs and nods. "But what are you going to do for money?"

"I'm not certain. I was thinking about working at Scores because it's close by." I'm a little tipsy after lunch. He leads me to his car, pulls out a checkbook from the console, and hands me a $7,000 check. "This is to hold you over until you figure it out." I've never had so much money in my life. I kiss him in front of my building, on the street, in full view of everyone. It's a long, passionate kiss that includes a lot of tongue. I start to wonder whether God has finally heard my requests for a sugar daddy. This, however, does not feel transactional, and I do not feel like a sugar baby. This feels genuine.

He finally calls, and we agree to meet for lunch the next day. I'm so nervous that I spend the entire night deciding what to wear. Nothing about me shouts "classy" or "sophisticated." All of my outfits resemble those of a high-class escort. I try on dozens of clothes before settling on a white knit tank top that falls low enough to reveal my ample cleavage, tight jeans, and a pair of thrifted Roberto Cavalli wooden platform wedges.

When I arrive at the restaurant, he is already seated at the table. He rises up as soon as he sees me and does not sit down again until I do. As his gaze moves across my body, collecting every detail, I blush. He lavishes me with so many compliments that I feel like the most beautiful, brilliant girl in the world when I'm with him. "I love the way you speak," he remarks. "It's very Italian." It's almost like a song." He's blown away by how well I speak Italian. "You must teach me!" he exclaims. When he finally asks how old I am, I lie and tell him I'm twenty, despite the fact that I'm only nineteen. I made the decision not to tell him I'm still in high school. That would raise a red signal for a man of this type, in my opinion.

As I eat my lunch, I can't help but notice the hostess's judgmental stares and ugly looks that I just seem to be getting. "So, what's your plan now that you're no longer working at the dungeon?" asked the man. "I'm not sure. To be perfectly honest, I just want to get a lousy automobile and go around the country seeing everything." He laughs and nods. "But what are you going to do for money?", "I'm not certain. I was thinking about working at Scores because it's close by."
I'm a little tipsy after lunch. He leads me to his car, pulls out a checkbook from the console, and hands me a $7,000 check. "This is to hold you over until you figure it out." I've never had so much money in my life. I kiss him in front of my building, on the street, in full view of everyone. It's a long, passionate kiss that includes a lot of tongue. I start to wonder whether God has finally heard my requests for a sugar daddy. This, however, does not feel transactional, and I do not feel like a sugar baby. This feels genuine.

A few days later, Rohan and I have lunch again, this time at a restaurant in the Financial District, where he works. He introduces me to the wait staff and the maître d', and unlike in the last place, none of them appear amused by the teenage girl dining with the older man. I can barely get a sentence out during lunch. Dozens of people approach our table to greet him, as if he were the Godfather. "This is my dear friend, the lovely Julia," he introduces himself. "She's from Milan." I nod and join in. He asks, seemingly out of nowhere, why I haven't paid the check yet. I pause for a moment. "I don't know, I don't want you to think I'm only here for your money," I go on to say.
He instantly turns it off. "I'm leaving for India for a couple of months and I don't want to worry about you." He reaches into his jacket, pulls out a wad of cash, and nonchalantly places it into my handbag under the table.

When I look over at the table beside us and see Jerry Springer seated less than five feet away, I can hardly contain myself. I recall a time when Jerry Springer was my sole source of entertainment. The audience members' soothing chorus of "Jerry! Jerry! Jerry!" drowned out the continuous noise in my head. He appears to be a completely different person when he isn't on a grimy stage, manipulating other people's drama. Rohan observes my expression and jokes, "Are you starstruck?" Feeling ashamed, I nod. "Do you want me to ask him for an autograph?" he jokes, a cheeky grin on his face. When I nod, he looks surprised. He returns a few moments later with a cocktail napkin bearing Jerry Springer's autograph. He sends me back to my modest studio in a large stretch limo after lunch. I'm pleased as I thumb through the crisp bills. I have a total of $10,000.

"We're rich!" I yell as I burst through the front door, waving the cash.

"We're wealthy!" I toss a few hundred-dollar bills at Liana. "Oh my God!" she screams as she rushes out of bed and hops up and down with me. "We're wealthy!" Later, as we lie side by side on the canopy bed, she says, "What kind of car does he drive?"

"I'm not sure." I believe it had a letter B on the steering wheel."

"Bugatti!"

"No."

"Bentley?"

"Yeah! That should do it."

"When do I get to meet him?"

"He's going away for a month." When he returns!"

We squeal with delight.

In his absence, Rohan and I text occasionally. A lot at first, then progressively less and less. I graduated from high school and decided to celebrate by getting high. With my father's assistance, I completed my drug program, and now I simply have to report to probation once a month to scan my hand.

Chapter 8:
PTSD

I drive through pouring rain and darkness to Harmony's residence in upstate New York, where she's been living with a heroin dealer for the past year. When I arrive, all of her belongings are in rubbish bags on the porch. When she sees my automobile, she laughs and rolls her eyes. "Whose grandmother did you rob?!" Harmony screams through the front door. "I got a good deal!" As she nervously whispers to her ex-boyfriend, I assist her in loading the endless boxes of loose pieces of paper, photo albums, and trinkets into the trunk. "Do we have to bring all this shit?" When she returns to the trunk with the last bag, I question her. "I don't trust him," she muffles. "What's his deal?"

When his silhouette approaches the doorway, she hushes me. I shift the subject as soon as she gives me the look. While we store the rest of her belongings in the driveway, he returns inside and closes the door. "Um, what's his problem?" I speak to her in hushed tones. "I'll tell you when we're in the car," she replies quietly. Once we're on the road, she admits, "It was getting really bad between us.", "What do you mean?", "He threw me on the ground and twisted my arm.", "What are you doing with him?" "How did you stop being a lesbian?"

She chuckles. "Yeah, I'm not sure. It was just getting lonely. So, where are we headed?"

"I have no fucking idea!" I exclaim, a mischievous grin on my face.

"Okay, sounds like fun," she says.

We drive all night and make it all the way to Tennessee when smoke begins to seep through the bonnet of the automobile. When the engine begins to sound like gunshots, I do my best to pull over to the side of the road. "Oh, that's it, the engine seized!" Harmony says as she peers into the smokey hood. "Fuck!!" I yell. We pause to glance at each other, then burst out laughing.

We shiver on the highway railing in the pouring rain, waiting for the tow truck for hours while amusing ourselves. We frighten each other with stories of serial killers. We concoct a complicated fiction about us being cousins through a family adoption. She uses her Notes app to practice the stand-up performance she's been working on. "I haven't laughed like this in a long time," I tell her, my pants soaked after peeing in them a few times. "Me too, dude." Her tone shifts. "You have no idea what I was going through."

"Could you please stop being so secretive?" "What the fuck happened?", "Okay, you have to promise not to tell anyone." She extends her pinkie, and I clasp it in mine. "I promise."

"I started shooting up again," she confesses. "I'm better now, but we were selling it.", "You were selling heroin?!", "He was! I was just trying to help him, but someone tipped off the FBI, who have been monitoring us for two months.", "Harmony! What is your name?!", "They even came to the house looking for guns but luckily we buried them in the lot next door." In disbelief, I listen to her. "I honestly believe you coming to get me out of nowhere is like God or something." "You genuinely saved my life." Tears well up in my eyes as I wrap my arms around her. "I love you," I say quietly.

We slept in a motel for the following three days while the automobile was being fixed. I've been told that locating the required vintage part could take weeks, and even then, it could be defective. We decided to abandon it in favor of renting a car to continue our journey. I instantly recall that my friend Brian recently relocated from the Midwest to Louisiana. "Let's go visit him!" I say.
Harmony seemed dissatisfied. "He's gay, don't worry.", "Fine, but you're driving."

We arrive in Louisiana's bayou after nine hours of uninterrupted driving. It's over a thousand miles away from Manhattan, and I like not being reminded of anything. We creep inside the tiny house in the middle of the night, and Brian is already asleep. It's a humid night, and the house lacks air conditioning, but I find comfort in the oppressive heat. Every time I step outside, I feel as if I'm being enveloped in a warm hug, which is exactly what I need.

When I wake up in the morning, I'm surprised to see a tall, lanky person uncomfortably standing in the doorway, waiting to be allowed in. "Umm, do you wanna come in?" I ask. He nods his head and smiles like a child. He enters the room and takes a seat at the foot of my bed. His pupils are the size of ants, and he appears tense and jittery. "You're so pretty," he remarks. "I'm Eric."

He extends his trembling, feeble hand, which is scribbled all over. His skin is burnt and oily, and he has poorly drawn tattoos all over his face. His tank top has holes and stains all over it, he has mosquito bites all over his body, and his arms exhibit the marks of a difficult existence. I shake his hand, and he places a crystal in the palm of my hand. Suddenly, I feel the ice layer that has been protecting my heart melt away. "This will protect you even when I'm not here."

I offer to drive him to the petrol station so he can grab a pack of cigarettes. He reaches for the aux cord once we're in the car. He begins his concert with "Lay Lady Lay" by Bob Dylan, then turns to Russian death rap before concluding with "Clair de lune" by Claude Debussy. I can see he enjoys everything by how thrilled he becomes. We drive past a shrimping boat that is slowly sinking and is covered in shattered furniture and waste bags. "Wow, that's so beautiful," he exhales.
I return my gaze to the boat. "Yeah, I guess it is." The sunset behind it, the contrast of the sea swallowing up the boat, and how poetic it all is strike me. "This little boat that worked so hard is gonna meet its fate, and there's nothing we can do about it," he said.

I enjoy being in Eric's company. Every day, I eagerly await his awakening in the room next door. On the bayou, there isn't much to do, yet Eric makes even the most ordinary tasks interesting. We race crabs, grill, and practice shooting cans with Brian's firearms. We investigate the abandoned houses that have been destroyed by years of hurricanes.

We paddle further into the Gulf than we expected one day when out in the canoe. The sky darkens, the wind kicks up, and the current pulls us further away from land. Eric instantaneously morphs into my protector when he sees the dread in my eyes. His sweet voice becomes heavy and solemn. He gently takes the paddle from my grasp and carefully returns us to land.

Doing things with Eric is like doing them for the first time. It's thrilling. He shows me the world through a fresh set of eyes, where everything, even the nasty, is gorgeous. When he goes into his room for hours to get high, I feel so lonely. He develops that glazed, empty look in his eyes, the classic hollow state of most heroin addicts. A part of me wants to join him on the cloud and feel what he's feeling, but I know how dangerous that path is for me. I make every effort to abstain for as long as possible.

I have to force him to look after himself. He despises showers because they remind him of the blood that poured down his legs and swirled down the drain after he was raped as a child by a stranger. He was a little boy who didn't know any better. He saw it as his "gay punishment." His Catholic background only reinforced this. As a result, he never told a soul. So we take baths instead. He enjoys it when I lather up his back and massage shampoo into his hair. I even get him some rubber ducks from Walmart. We're giggling like two tiny kids, like brother and sister. It's also as if I'm his mother. And it's as if he's my mother at times. But he enjoys being my sis the best when I let him wear my lingerie and photograph him. He enjoys posing provocatively as I encourage him.

As I listen to his terrible stories, I am in wonder. "When I was twelve, I shot heroin for the first time in the back of a trailer with my friend's older brother." My first love was him. He was nineteen years old when he took my virginity. When he said, 'I ain't no faggot,' and stopped talking to me, I was distraught. I started tricking the IHOP after that, but as I got older and my voice got deeper, they didn't want me anymore." I play the role of a therapist to him, encouraging and soothing him. "You're aware that none of this is your fault, right?" You must cease punishing yourself." He gives a nod. "I know, you're right."

I read to him at night from our favorite book, The Outsiders. I call him Ponyboy, and he refers to me as Cherry. We even used a syringe to tattoo it on each other. I poked his arm with a stick, and he put a cherry on my buttocks. Brian was enraged by this. He screamed at Eric not to ruin my life. Brian and Harmony dislike our friendship. "Eric, Eric, Eric, Eric." Eric is in charge of everything!" Harmony is upset. "You can hang out with us if you want," I say. "You don't have to stay in your room sniffing pills by yourself!" She sighs and proceeds to microwave her fish-flavored tofu sticks.

Harmony and I outstay your welcome at Brian's place for a month and move into an old house on stilts at the end of a long, narrow lane that goes far out onto the Gulf. The entire house sways back and forth when the wind blows. We bought a Lincoln Town Car for $1500 from a neighbor who had fire ants crawling on his toes and blood leaking down his legs during the transaction. We get to know everyone and our neighbors invite us over for shrimp dinners. We spent Thanksgiving with the family of a guy we met at a pub. We go fishing off the coast of Mexico with random strangers and then enjoy the best barbecue we've ever had.

Harmony frequently hitchhikes to the nearest bar, where I frequently see her later playing billiards with the elderly. "I could honestly live here forever," she says, smiling. "Me, too," I admit. It's just another average afternoon as I round the bend on the long, winding road surrounded by water, on my way to the laundromat 20 minutes away. When the big old Town Car I'm driving loses control, spinning in circles and heading straight for the sea, I'm singing along to Fleetwood Mac's "The Chain," nodding my head to the music. As the automobile wraps itself around a large wooden telephone pole, I close my eyes and grab the steering wheel.

The impact is powerful, and the sound of metal crushing on wood reverberates throughout the room. The small plastic cigarette cup containing the remains of last weekend's vodka beverage flies away, spraying the entire backseat. The automobile smells strongly of booze and ashes, and my clothing are soiled. Panic comes in as I try to get out of the car, but the door is stuck shut. I had no choice but to exit the passenger door and change my clothing on the side of the road.

I call Harmony, who is too far away to walk over. I have no choice but to phone Brian and inform him of what has occurred. He's been unhappy with me for disrupting his and Eric's music sessions, and I'm embarrassed to contact him now, but he doesn't hesitate. I see his large green vehicle coming down the road in a few minutes.

Brian makes a joke when he gets out of the truck, which puts me at ease. Despite the oddness, I realize I am fortunate to have him. And I'm grateful to be alive because if it hadn't been for the pole, the car would have crashed into the bayou and I would have become alligator meal.

Printed in Great Britain
by Amazon